CHARMED BRACELETS

TRACEY ZABAR

charmed BRACELETS

with JENNIFER CEGIELSKI
foreword by LISA BIRNBACH
photographs by ELLEN SILVERMAN

STEWART, TABORI & CHANG
NEW YORK

TO DAVID, BENJAMIN, DANIEL, MICHAEL, WILLIAM, AND MUM AND DADDY, WITH LOVE.

AND REBECCA MARY ROSE, OUR BABY.

CONTENTS

my life in charm bracelets

BY LISA BIRNBACH

I LIKE CHARMS, BUT I LOVE CHARM BRACELETS. AND TO BE PER-FECTLY HONEST, UNLESS I'M PUTTING A CHARM BRACELET TOGETHER, IT WOULDN'T EVEN OCCUR TO ME TO LOOK FOR A NEW CHARM. BUT SHOW ME A DANGLING CHARM BRACELET SPARKLING AROUND A WRIST, AND I'M A GONER! IT NEVER FAILS. LIKE PEARLS, CIRCLE PINS, SIGNET RINGS, AND SIMPLE STUD EARRINGS (IN THE EAR-LOBES, THAT IS), CHARM BRACELETS ARE CLASSICS. THAT'S ONE OF THE REASONS I ENJOY THEM. THEY FEMINIZE A SPORTY JEANS-AND-T-SHIRT OUTFIT AND LEND THE HIP OUTFIT A SOMETIMES LONGED-FOR VINTAGE EDGE. THEY GO EXCELLENTLY WITH BLACK.

A CHARM BRACELET FEELS LIKE VALUE-ADDED JEWELRY. THERE'S THE SATISFYING FEEL AND LOOK OF THE LINKS AND THE CLASP, PLUS THE PERSONALIZED PLEASURE OF A MEANINGFUL CHARM. THEN ANOTHER.

A CHARMING GOLD BRACELET. (LISA BIRNBACH)

Now with two or three charming charms attached, you get the bonus of the musical jingle. That's a lot to get from a bauble, I think.

My mother never wore a standard charm bracelet, but until she was robbed during a family vacation in London, she did own a unique length of heavy eighteen-karat rope with the tiny plastic beads from her three baby bracelets encased in gold with the occasional diamond, ruby, and turquoise detail. I can't do it justice, but it was original, had my brothers' and my names suspended from it, and was therefore more or less a charm bracelet. I hope the thief has a son named Norman.

Once in the basement of my maternal grandparents' home, I found a tarnished silver charm bracelet in a box of mementos. The charms were utilitarian: a wheelbarrow, a washing board, a pair of scissors, but only half survived (the scis or the sors, I'm not certain). You get the idea. This bracelet was good for you but no fun at all. It reminded the wearer of chores to be done, a strange motif for jewelry, I've always thought.

My father bought me my first charm bracelet. I got to go to the store with him. It felt a little rushed, but we assembled most of it right on the spot. I got the preteen's requisite ballet shoes, tennis racket, and, since this was the seventies, Mad Money. Anyway it wouldn't have been a charm bracelet if it had had just one charm on it.

I offered to write the foreword to Tracey Zabar's book because Tracey reintroduced me to the delights of charm bracelets. I started to notice her pretty and amusing bracelets at New York's tonier shops and realized you could design a bracelet around a theme, a passion, or just pile on the charms. Within the last few years I had been working on a gold

THE "SCIS" "SORS" BRACELET.
(LISA BIRNBACH)

bracelet, but it had gone wrong, just wrong, and I didn't enjoy wearing it and so I didn't. Tracey came to the rescue. Very calmly, like the patient diagnostician she is, she analyzed my problem: not enough charms, not enough color, and some feng shui (not really, but why not call it that?) that could be easily addressed. Now that charm bracelet is doing fine and is a frequent chosen companion. Meanwhile, I saw a glamorous photograph of one of Tracey's Paris bracelets in *Town & Country,* and since it was seriously cheaper than a trip to France, I sprung for that too. Now I'm collecting charms for my daughters' bracelets-to-be. I'm very happy to bask in Tracey Zabar's charming world.

Which gets us to my last point: Charm bracelets are not just for enjoying now, they're for later on too. You know what I mean. Not to be macabre, but they can be so extremely personalized that they can tell your history almost as well as your DNA. I said almost. You've seen bracelets with diplomas, children's silhouettes, souvenir charms of resort islands (some with sand), miniaturized trophies, all with informative engraving. If you get to wear your grandma's charm bracelet, you get to know your grandma during an earlier time in her life. That's nice. (By the way, I'm not going to wear that silver household appliance bracelet anytime soon, but it does make me feel closer to my forebears.)

So, go find that family heirloom, or start one yourself and shake your wrist!

INTRODUCTION

the appeal of charms

THERE IS SOMETHING INNATELY CHARMING ABOUT A CHARM BRACELET. SOME PEOPLE MIGHT LOVE THE SIGNATURE JINGLE AND JANGLE SUCH A BRACELET MAKES WHEN THE WEARER IS IN MOTION, WHILE OTHERS ENJOY THE FACT THAT YOU REALLY NEED TO GET UP CLOSE AND PERSONAL TO EXAMINE EACH QUIRKY LITTLE CHARM DANGLING FROM THE LINKS. BUT FOR ME, THE MOST IRRESISTIBLE AND ALLURING THING ABOUT A CHARM BRACELET IS ITS ABILITY TO TELL A STORY UNIQUE TO ITS OWNER. CONSIDER A CHARM BRACELET "HISTORY ON A WRIST"—THERE IS NOTHING MORE PERSONAL OR SYMBOLIC. LADEN WITH TINY FIGURINES, FOND REMEMBRANCES, AND SWEET FORGET-ME-NOTS COLLECTED OVER THE YEARS, CHARM BRACELETS

MY FAVORITE BRACELET. A MAGNIFICENT GROUPING OF GOLD, ENAMEL, DIA-MOND, GEM, AND PEARL CHARMS, PLUS REVERSE-PAINTED GLASS INTAGLIOS, TIN-TYPES, AND MAD MONEY CHARMS. SOME "MECHANICALS" OF NOTE: A TOILET ENGRAVED "HIS" AND "HERS," A DOCTOR'S BAG WITH MINI MEDICAL TOOLS, A HULA GIRL WITH SWAYING CHAIN SKIRT, AND OLD BLUE EYES HIMSELF. (TRACEY ZABAR)

chronicle small moments in a life lived. Truly, to wear one is to wear your history upon your sleeve.

And while the adornments women choose have always been an expression of personal style, few ornaments, barring the engagement ring, have held as dear a place in women's hearts—or create as big a commotion, both literally and figuratively—as the charm bracelet. Walk down the street wearing one, and a woman will stop you in your tracks to share stories about her own treasured charm bracelet, her mother's, or even her grandmother's. Charm bracelets encourage a connection. Like quilts or samplers, they are a woman's art and such a "girl thing."

Jewelry advertises the wearer's status and social standing—her power, position, and wealth. It is a way to flaunt, to be fashionable, seductive, or elegant. For its part, the charm bracelet is an oh-so-feminine autobiography on a chain. Charm bracelets express who a woman is in a subtle way, simultaneously giving a whimsical little nod to her style while also serving as a record of remembrance of her life.

In the most literal sense of the word, charms work magic on the viewer. They can be feminine or funny, glamorous or girlish, classic or kitschy. Though tiny in their proportions, these sweet tokens make a grand statement about the wearer's taste and humor. "To charm" also means to attract, and these bracelets do exactly that. They draw the eye to one's wrist, where a compelling tale unfolds. And if

THE BRACELET THAT STARTED IT ALL, BEGUN IN 1947 BY MY FATHER FOR MY MOTHER. MOST OF THE CHARMS ARE MECHANICALS THAT REVEAL A SURPRISE INSIDE. THOUGHT TO HAVE BEEN STOLEN IN 1965, IT MIRACULOUSLY RESURFACED IN A BAG OF A LITTLE GIRL'S DRESS-UP JEWELRY FIFTEEN YEARS LATER. MY MOTHER WEARS IT TO THIS DAY. (MARY BLUMENREICH)

modern-day charms don't cast spells in the ancient sense, they do contain a powerful force: memory, in the form of personal history.

My own love affair with charm bracelets began ages ago with an heirloom I coveted. Alas, it was unobtainable to me back then, but it sparked a fire within that hasn't stopped burning since. Determined to wear a charm bracelet I loved, I set out to make my own. The first time I wore one, a woman begged me to sell it to her right off my wrist, right there in the middle of a New York City bus. After that, anytime I wore one of my bracelets, fabulous, gorgeous women, young and old, insisted on giving me their telephone numbers and taking mine in the hopes of acquiring a bracelet. Soon I realized I had struck an emotional goldmine and hurried to make four more charm bracelets, which became the beginning of my very first jewelry collection for the store Barneys New York. A business was born, and I became a jewelry designer.

I wear a charm bracelet nearly every day now—I have dozens—and people still stop me on the street to chat about whichever one I'm wearing or share tales of bracelets they have known, loved, or lost. Their enchanting and sentimental stories still give me goose bumps. I hope you'll feel the same way about the bracelets you see on these pages.

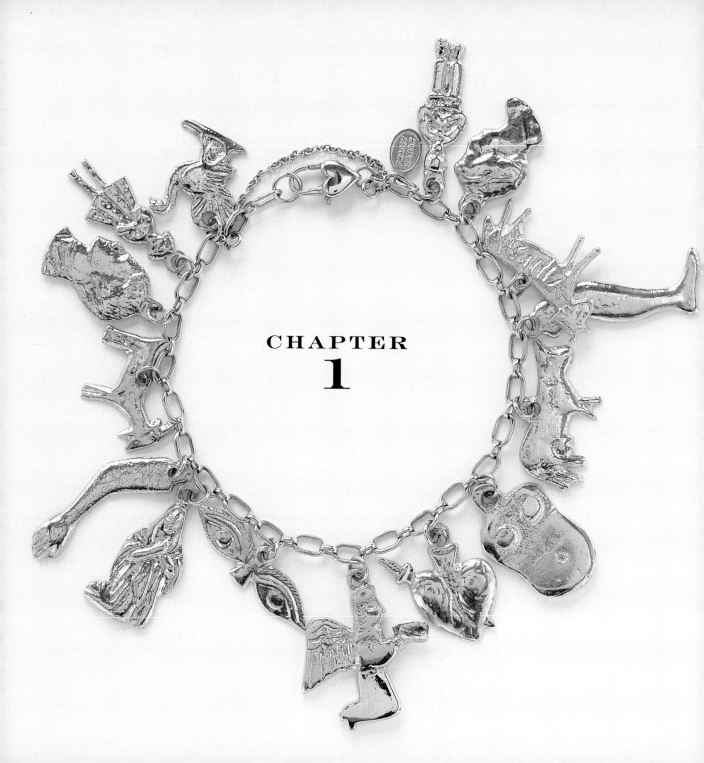

CHAPTER
1

A *charmed* HISTORY

CHARM BRACELETS, IN ONE FORM OR ANOTHER, CAN BE FOUND
IN ALMOST EVERY ERA OF JEWELRY HISTORY. PEOPLE SEEM TO
HAVE ALWAYS HAD THE NEED TO ADORN THEMSELVES WITH BEAUTIFUL,
SYMBOLIC, OR MAGICAL THINGS. NO DOUBT THE VERY FIRST WOMAN TO
PICK UP SOME SHINY OBJECT AND TUCK IT INTO HER MATTED HAIR WAS
THE ONE WHO STARTED IT ALL.

ANCIENT PEOPLES RELIED UPON AMULETS AND OTHER LUCKY CHARMS
TO WARD OFF THE "EVIL EYE" AND OTHER BAD SPIRITS, AND THEN THEY
HELD FAST TO RELIGIOUS CHARMS PROMISING FERTILITY AND LOVE.
WHEN IT CAME TO BAUBLES AND ADORNMENTS, RELIGION AND MAGIC

A FINE COLLECTION OF GOLD MILAGROS. COMMONLY MADE OF CHEAP METALS,
MILAGROS ARE SOLD FOR PENNIES OUTSIDE CHURCHES IN LATIN AMERICA, WHERE
THE FAITHFUL PIN THEM ONTO SAINTS' STATUES TO PETITION FOR GOOD LUCK. I
KNOW OF A CHURCH WHERE THE PRIESTS REMOVE THE MILAGROS AND RESELL
THEM TO THE VENDORS OUTSIDE...A WHOLE ECONOMIC ECOSYSTEM FUELED BY
CHARMS! (TRACEY ZABAR)

A TIMELESS ENGRAVED HEART LOCKET. (VICTORIA & ALBERT MUSEUM)

were often intertwined. Wishes and prayers were inscribed on minia-ture scrolls and tucked into little cases. Special jewelry was worn to pass into the afterlife. Offerings or tokens were given to protect humans and livestock from disease. Talismans in every imaginable form of jewelry were designed to be worn on the wrist, from the ears, in the hair, around the neck, and close to the heart. Decorated religious reliquaries housed tiny pieces of bones alleged to have come from saints. Saints' images were embellished with gems on Russian icons. Women through the ages carried rosary beads, worry beads, and love beads as magical artifacts. Medieval gold love jew-els were rife with symbolism: hearts indicated love; ivy the "clinging" nature of women; pearls, tears.

By the 1700s and 1800s, personalized and miniaturized jewels were all the rage, particularly among the royal and rich. Members of the nobility indicated their status by wearing impressive seals and symbols of royal orders. The wealthy treasured "miniatures," tiny paintings of loved ones on pendants, bracelets, or pins. Precursors to photographs, these mementos were exchanged between lovers, worn to honor a loved one away at war, or commissioned to docu-ment the members of a family. Little decorated vinaigrettes filled with smelling salts dangled from rings in case a lady of good breeding found herself feeling faint in the presence of company. Intricate, tiny mosaics on bracelets and necklaces com-memorated visits to exotic locales, and intaglios gained popularity.

A PRICELESS PLATINUM, DIA-MOND, GOLD, AND PEARL CHARM BRACELET, COLLECTED OVER MANY YEARS. MANY OF THE CHARMS ARE LUCKY, INCLUDING TWO OF THE NUMBER THIRTEEN. MOST ARE DIA-MOND PAVÉ, AND THERE IS ALSO A CALIBRÉ-CUT CHARM OF A PERSON HOLDING THE NUMBERS 1938. (TERRY RODGERS AND MELODY)

A WONDERFUL GOLD BRACELET COLLECTED BY THE OWNER'S GRAND-MOTHER. ONE CHARM BELONGED TO HER LATE FATHER-IN-LAW. IT BEARS THE INSCRIPTION "DUTCH TREAT CLUB," WHOSE MEMBERS ALWAYS PAID FOR THEIR OWN LUNCHES. ENGRAVED ON THE REVERSE WITH "VICTOR BORGE," THE CHARM WAS HIS LIFETIME ACHIEVEMENT AWARD IN THE CLUB. (PAULA BORGE)

TOP: THIS SILVER BRACELET IS A COPY OF A PLATINUM ORIGINAL MADE IN THE LATE 1920S, POSSIBLY BY CARTIER. THE CHARM WITH THE COLORED PASTE STONES SIGNIFIES "MY DEAREST"—THE FIRST LETTER OF EACH STONE SPELLS IT OUT (DIAMOND, EMERALD, AMETHYST, RUBY, EMERALD, SAPPHIRE, TOPAZ). (ROBIN DEUTSCH) BOTTOM: A STERLING BRACELET WITH PASTE CHARMS, POSSIBLY GERMAN, CIRCA 1925–1930. THE BEAUTIFULLY CRAFTED CHARMS ARE SUSPENDED FROM LONG, OVAL JUMP RINGS. (ROBIN DEUTSCH)

Chatelaines—useful brooches with scaled-down sewing tools or charmlike trinkets such as keys, watch, and magnifying glass attached by fine chains—were pinned to a woman's waist to keep essentials at the ready. Georgian women had fine copies of their jewels made in paste. Tiny and twinkling was the fashion, from "en tremblant" tiaras shimmering in the light to the one-of-a-kind enameled Fabergé eggs on the bracelet of the ill-fated Russian Czarina Alexandra.

Those ever-repressed Victorians were mad for jewelry coyly hinting at their romantic relationships. Bracelets were particularly important; the fashion was to wear more than one at a time on each wrist. Some bracelets were woven of hair, and little charms encased tiny locks snipped from a lover's head. A piece of men's jewelry, such as a beloved's watch fob, might be appropriated and transformed into a pendant to hang from a chain around a lady's neck. Engravings offered besotted pleadings to "remember me when this you see." Sometimes the gems themselves conveyed a hidden message—the first initial of each stone would spell out an endearment. For example, a ring set with a ruby, emerald, garnet, amethyst, ruby, and diamond would indicate the somewhat lukewarm REGARD; and a piece sporting lapis-lazuli, opal, vermeil (the old name for garnet), and emerald promised LOVE for those most worthy. Rings of the time might have hidden compartments within which to tuck a minuscule memento. Following the loss of her beloved husband Albert, trend-setting Queen Victoria started the craze for mourning jewelry crafted with tiny remembrances (she also liked to wear a bracelet made of linked miniatures of all her children). Meanwhile, across the pond, tiny tintypes

A PRE-1920 RUSSIAN BRACE-LET, WITH SIX ENAMELED EGG CHARMS (POSSIBLY FABERGÉ) SUS-PENDED FROM A LOVELY HANDMADE CHAIN. THERE IS ALSO A GOLD ELEPHANT WITH A PINK SAPPHIRE EYE, A ROSE GOLD LLAMA, AND A VERY BEAUTIFUL CIRCLE CHARM WITH FLOWERS GROWING AROUND A WILD BOAR OR PIG. (FRED LEIGHTON)

of boys heading off to the Civil War were hidden in their sweethearts' lockets. Later, sassy suffragettes wore pins in the shape of gates with symbolic locks, as well as jewelry with green (G), white (W), and violet (V) gems—a silent protest chant to "Give Women the Vote."

It wasn't long before the first rumblings of charm bracelets as we know them today began to be felt. The stylish Art Deco era, a major period for jewelry that set the cornerstone for modern designs, saw gorgeous bracelets featuring dangling elements. These early examples usually were designed with gems set in platinum and featured thin, sleek charms that were often one-sided. Diamonds sparkled alone or mixed with emeralds, rubies, sapphires, amethysts, and pearls. Then the world was at war for the second time, and the importance of "sweetheart" mementos and jewels came into play. As the conflict approached, families smuggled their little gold heirlooms out of Europe. In the trenches, coins were fashioned into art, crudely engraved with messages of love. Back home, women wore inexpensive jewelry proclaiming their status as a sweetheart, sister, or wife of a soldier. Medals were pinned on in remembrance of lives lost. Military motifs made their way into jewelry of the era—airplanes, miniature servicemen, Stars and Stripes. Jacqueline Cochran, the first woman to pilot a bomber across the North Atlantic, was photographed in 1941 wearing a lucky bracelet with thirteen charms— she never made a flight without it.

A SORORITY AND FRATERNITY CHARM BRACELET, COLLECTED BETWEEN 1946 AND 1948 AT PENN STATE, BY MONA AND NORTON BERNSTEIN. (JUDY BERNSTEIN BUNZL)

TOP: A GOLD BRACELET WITH SIX BEAUTIFUL ANTIQUE INTAGLIO STONE SEALS. (JOY TOBACK-GALICKI AND MYRON TOBACK) BOTTOM: FIVE ANTIQUE WATCH FOBS, EACH WITH STONE INTAGLIO SEAL. THE CHARMS ON BOTH OF THESE BRACELETS WERE COLLECTED BY ELAINE TOBACK. (JOY TOBACK-GALICKI AND MYRON TOBACK)

The charm craze was further fueled by the increasingly influential worlds of fashion and celebrity, spread through the mass media via magazines and movies. Madcap clothing designer Elsa Schiaparelli allegedly had a passion for jangly bracelets and watch fobs, and eternal sartorial icon Coco Chanel hung her jewelry with clinking coins. Notorious rivals, these designers were both fans of the concept of piling jewelry on in abundance. Chanel's coin bracelets struck a chord, thanks to either their implication of riches or simply their charm, and the look was quickly picked up by style-setters like Lauren Bacall, who wore one for a *Harper's Bazaar* photo shoot in 1944. Hollywood stars of the day clanged through many a movie wearing loud, luxe charm bracelets. A more playful interpretation was found in the brightly colored Bakelite fruit designs featuring dangling cherries, oranges, and more.

The 1950s marked the golden years. Charm bracelets perfectly complemented the three-quarter-length sleeves in vogue (all the better to show off your collection of charms!) as well as the ladylike image portrayed by Dior's noteworthy "New Look." Etiquette books reminded women to match their jewelry to their wardrobe, and also to their man (really!). It seemed as though every woman had to have a charm bracelet—and, in fact, every woman could. While the most valuable examples were made of platinum or higher karat gold (usually fourteen or eighteen karat) with precious or semiprecious stones, everyday charm bracelets were made of affordable base metals, often called pot metal, as well as sterling silver and nine- and ten-karat gold.

A MAGNIFICENT, HEAVY GOLD AND STONE CHARM BRACELET, INHERITED FROM A BELOVED GRAND-MOTHER. (DR. CATHY RADUNS)

22

the charm of popular culture

MUSIC AND BOOKS

Once charm bracelets became mainstream, they began to reflect everything in pop culture. Some celebrities may have worn charms, but some became charms themselves on kitschy bracelets throughout the 1950s and 1960s.

MUSIC

Those with a passion for tickling the ivories could sport a Liberace charm bracelet, complete with piano and candelabra.

Ladies could proclaim their love for the King by donning an Elvis charm bracelet, circa 1956, which featured a guitar, a broken heart for "Heartbreak Hotel," a hound dog, and an Elvis photo to swoon over.

Little dangling heads of the Fab Four Beatles, as well as their less famous (and arguably less talented) brethren the Monkees, also appeared on charm bracelets. Who can resist a whole wristful of cuties?

BOOKS

Published in 1936, the thirteenth book in the popular Nancy Drew series was *The Mystery of the Ivory Charm*. In the story, Nancy investigates a suspect circus and whether an ivory elephant charm really protects its wearer from harm.

LEFT: THE BEATLES HIT THE NOT-SO-BIG SCREEN, WITH A PHOTOGRAPH IN A TELEVISION CHARM FROM THE 1960S. (TRACEY ZABAR) RIGHT: HEY HEY WE'RE THE MONKEES. A FAUX GOLD CHARM BRACELET WITH PHOTOGRAPHS OF THE SEMI-FAB FOUR FROM THE 1960S POP GROUP. (TRACEY ZABAR)

Some bracelets and charms were made of inexpensive metals plated to look like silver or gold. A magazine feature from the era exclaimed, "There's a charm for every woman, whether her purse affords fifty cents for twinkling nickel or hundreds of dollars for gold and gems." I couldn't agree more.

In their heyday, thousands of bracelets were lovingly assembled with meaningful charms. Little endearments were collected for each love affair. Rose petals and rice tossed at weddings were stored in miniature vials. Smooth shards of beach glass and tiny bottles of sand recalled memories of lazy summer days and that perfect honeymoon. Birthdays were duly noted each year with a new addition to the links. Charms paid tribute to the admirable careers of the day—wife, mother, teacher, nurse, stewardess. Fathers rewarded mothers with a charm for each child born, and, later, others to announce each grandchild. Club ladies collected awards, for social service, pounds lost, or years spent on the wagon. The quiet moments of life were commemorated.

Women whose own mothers and grandmothers had never left the farm or shtetl began to go abroad. Descendants of immigrants who had taken one long trip in steerage were now ladies on the grand tour. Souvenir travel charms boasted of these trips around the world—or, more locally, around the state. Coin bracelets evolved into "luckies" featuring gambling charms, poker chips, and icons like rabbits' feet, roulette wheels, and four-leaf clovers. Charms started to develop a sense of humor— dollar bills and pound sterling notes were

YOU LUCKY GIRL, YOU. THIS FABULOUS BRACELET FEATURES BAKELITE AND SILVER GAMBLING CHIPS FROM MONACO. (TRACEY ZABAR)

A STERLING SILVER BRACELET WITH CHARMS COLLECTED DURING AND FOLLOWING WORLD WAR II. THE ENAMELED SHIELD CHARMS REPRESENT TOWNS IN ENGLAND. (TRACEY ZABAR)

the charm of popular culture

TELEVISION AND MOVIES

TELEVISION

The characters from the television series *Bewitched* were pictured on a bracelet inside a charm shaped like a television set.

Fans of the series *The Beverly Hillbillies* (you know who you are) relished a charm bracelet featuring photos of Uncle Jed, Jethro, Granny, Elly May, and the whole gang in the family jalopy.

Admirers of hunky Vince Edwards, star of the 1960s series *Ben Casey,* could show their solidarity for the TV doctor by wearing a charm bracelet with the symbols for "man, woman, birth, death, infinity" (the opening narrative to every show) on it.

Hearts dangled from the links of *I Love Lucy* charm bracelets worn by little girls.

The television show *This Is Your Life* often presented charm bracelets to female guests who appeared on the show and told the story of their lives and careers.

The character of Alice, played by Audrey Meadows on the television series *The Honeymooners,* sometimes sported a big, clunky charm bracelet or two.

THE MOVIES

The 1963 Doris Day movie *Move Over, Darling* had an amusing running joke throughout the story about two very loud, clanging charm bracelets (worn by the actress Polly Bergen) that drove a judge, and everyone else in the courtroom, mad.

A sweet little charm bracelet featuring sweet little Shirley Temple was first made by Monocraft (and later by Monet).

"COME AND LISTEN TO MY STORY 'BOUT A MAN NAMED JED..." A WHIMSICAL *BEVERLY HILLBILLIES* BRACELET. (TRACEY ZABAR)

YES, I AM A HOUSEWIFE. TOP: TWO BRACELETS OF 1950S ADVERTISING CHARMS THAT ORIGINALLY SOLD FOR ONE DOLLAR, PLUS TWENTY CENTS POSTAGE. (TRACEY ZABAR) BOTTOM: GIVE ME CANDY, GIVE ME TOYS, GIVE ME EVERYTHING. A CONTEMPORARY CANDY BRACELET, WITH PLASTIC CHARMS. YUM. (MY GENERATION)

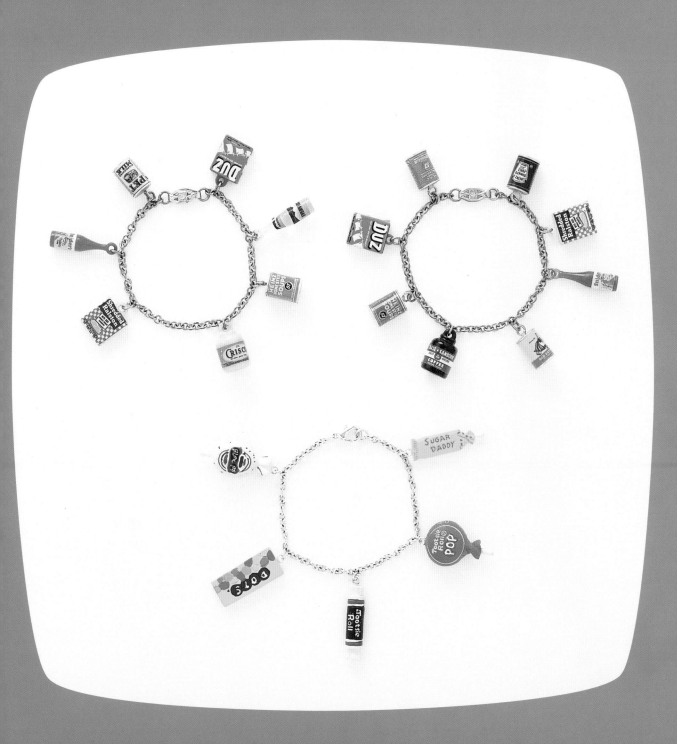

tucked into little boxes marked "In case of emergency, break glass," and moving charms with secret messages such as "Kiss me" or the cheeky "Go to Hell" were collected. If you take a close look at vintage charms from this period, you'll see they often serve as time capsules for the aspirations and lifestyle of a bygone era, preserved for posterity. I've seen charms that represented the family rec-room bar, from kitschy bar stools to little liquor bottles, as well as a miniature split-level house that opened to show an immaculate *Leave-It-to-Beaver*-esque living room set within. I've even seen a charm depicting a perfect enameled chicken on a rotisserie that actually spins—probably an homage to some unknown 1950s housewife, who undoubtedly perfected her *Joy of Cooking,* much to the delight of her mister.

The torch was passed to the next generation as parents bought a child-sized bracelet to celebrate the birth of a daughter and presented her with a new charm each year. Girls eagerly signed up to receive a series of twelve charms from charm-of-the-month clubs, or saved up their babysitting money to buy themed charms in honor of wholesome hobbies like bowling and scouting. Little girls took trips with their parents around the country and brought home souvenir booty like a bucking bronco charm from the Wild West or mini Statue of Liberty from the Big Apple to hang from their bracelets. Suburban teenyboppers sported bracelets with images of their favorite crooners and music idols, television shows, and cartoons. Cheerleaders and

TOP: A CHICKEN IN EVERY POT, A CHARM BRACELET ON EVERY WRIST. (TRACEY ZABAR) BOTTOM: A FINE GOLD AND ENAMEL BRACELET, PROPERTY OF A YOUNG LADY. (JULIA ALGE)

the charm of popular culture

ANIMATION AND CURRENT EVENTS

ANIMATION

The sailor who was "strong to the finich," Popeye, was featured on a magic picture charm bracelet.

Fans of Bedrock could meet the Flintstones on a silver charm bracelet with 3-D figures of Fred, Wilma, Pebbles, Dino, and Barney Rubble, and his son BamBam. (Betty, where are you?)

Although most pop culture charm bracelets were kitschy and relatively inexpensive, there are some notable exceptions. In the early 1940s, Cartier and Disney collaborated on some real jewelry featuring Disney characters. These bracelets are a meaningful missing link between cheap character bracelets and the fabulous, priceless platinum and gemstone bracelets of the same period (many of which were made by Cartier).

CURRENT EVENTS

Multiple births were merchandised with the debut of a charm bracelet featuring each of the Dionne quints, the five identical sisters born in rural Ontario, Canada, in 1934 who became a media sensation. The bracelet was made by Monocraft (and later by Monet).

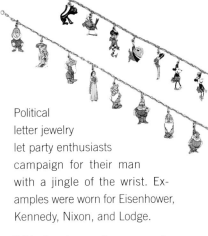

Political letter jewelry let party enthusiasts campaign for their man with a jingle of the wrist. Examples were worn for Eisenhower, Kennedy, Nixon, and Lodge.

With the dawn of space exploration in the 1960s came a charm bracelet to commemorate the giant leap for mankind made by the landing on the moon.

Company products or mascots such as Mr. Peanut often found their way onto inexpensive promotional charm bracelets.

LEFT: FLINTSTONES BRACELET. (TRACEY ZABAR) RIGHT: TWO DISNEY-CARTIER GOLD AND ENAMEL CHARM BRACELETS. (CHRISTIE'S)

🐾 I CRY FOR YOU. (TRACEY ZABAR)

🐾 A BRACELET WITH CHARMS RECEIVED AS GIFTS FOR THE OWNER'S BIRTHDAYS FROM AGE SIX TO SIXTEEN DURING THE LATE 1950S TO THE LATE 1960S INCLUDING A WHEEL OF SWISS CHEESE, A COCKER SPANIEL NAMED LICORICE, AND A PINK ENAMEL BIRTHDAY CAKE. THE MAD MONEY CHARM STOWED AN EMERGENCY DOLLAR FOR GETTING HOME WHEN THE OWNER STARTED DATING. (KAREN SACKS GLANTERNIK)

bobby soxers collected silver charms of high school moments—schoolbooks, penny loafers, footballs. The chatelaines of old evolved into sweater pins. Campus coeds donned bracelets with sorority and fraternity pins and Phi Beta Kappa keys as the never-take-it-off accessory to go with their saddle shoes, poodle skirts, and sweater twin sets. Best friends always knew what to get one another for that perfect birthday present.

Prefab charm bracelets known as "letter jewelry" spelled out nicknames like P-R-I-N-C-E-S-S, S-W-E-E-T-I-E-P-I-E, or H-O-N-E-Y in individual letter charms for young girls; a perfume advertisement from 1957 shows a version announcing "I-N-D-I-S-C-R-E-E-T" for those girls old enough to know better. Letter jewelry also took a political turn, declaring the patriotic message G-O-D-B-L-E-S-S-A-M-E-R-I-C-A or proclaiming the wearer's preference for a particular candidate, say K-E-N-N-E-D-Y or E-I-S-E-N-H-O-W-E-R.

My own memories of those salad days are filled with images of well-groomed ladies with beauty parlor hair, most of whom looked like a blurry hometown imitation of a first lady. Women wouldn't dare go out in public without a hat, gloves, and a nice suit. Everyone was expected to behave a certain way. Though I do miss how polite society was back then, the constrictions of that time thankfully no longer exist. Women were locked in prefeminist lives, but they still had stories to tell. It was all so very Mamie Eisenhower. More was more.

THE END OF AN OBSESSION

Then suddenly, it all stopped. The times were a-changing, and the seemingly insatiable charm bracelet craze that exploded across the nation right after World War II ended abruptly with the 1960s and the women's movement of the 1970s. The formerly respectable homemaker goals of marriage and motherhood were left behind in favor of high-powered careers and "finding yourself." So important to women's rights, this era of mods, hippies, and career girls was the death knell to these oh-so-girly bracelets. Even fashion was on a whole new track. A young woman who received a charm bracelet for her sweet sixteen birthday would never, ever dream of wearing it with her embroidered peasant shirt, ripped bellbottoms, and fringed leather jacket. Ladylike was out, free love was in, and the generation gap had widened—Mum and Dad clearly didn't know me at all.

Modern women didn't want or need these outmoded tokens of girlhood, and thousands of charm bracelets got buried in the bottom of jewelry boxes or family vaults and forgotten. Sisters no longer fought over Grandmother's bracelet, and Grandmother no longer wore a little silhouette charm of each grandchild, complete with engraved names and birth dates. Datebooks were now needed to remember those birthdays, because grandmothers were busy working, and so was Mommy. We really weren't getting married and having babies anymore anyway (well, I was, but that's a different story), and besides, dangly jewelry was a nuisance at the office, getting caught in typewriters and photocopy machines. And when the price of gold and silver rose through the stratosphere in the early 1980s, many neglected charm bracelets were either stolen or pawned or sold for scrap to be melted down and lost forever. Charm bracelets were, in a word, out.

CHARMS FROM A REMARKABLE LIFE. THE OWNER OF THIS BRACE-LET WAS A FOUNDER OF MS. MAGA-ZINE. ONE OF THE CHARMS WAS A GIFT FROM GLORIA STEINEM AND ANOTHER WAS A TYPEWRITER TO CELEBRATE HER FIRST BOOK. (LETTY COTTIN POGREBIN)

PEACE, BABY. A FABULOUS, STRIKING BRACELET, BOUGHT IN GREENWICH VILLAGE FOR FOUR DOLLARS. (AMY NEDERLANDER)

charming sayings

Charmed, I'm sure

The third time's the charm

Simply charming

Totally charming

Positively charming

Such a charmer

Hidden charms

Charm me

Baltimore, the charm city

Snake charmer

Charm school

Works like a charm

Charms of youth

She used her womanly charms

Music has charms to soothe the
  savage breast

How charming

A charmed life

You are my lucky charm

Charm the pants (or socks) off him

It's alarming how charming I feel

THE LONG-AWAITED REBIRTH

Now we've come full circle, and charm bracelets are hot again. Why? Perhaps we can chalk it up to embracing a sense of nostalgia, a revival of retro style, a need to have something undeniably personal again in a fast-changing, impersonal world, and, perhaps most importantly, a new comfortableness with who we are as women. From a fashion perspective, the charm bracelet looks great again as women discover their own sense of style without feeling like they have to adhere to a singular aesthetic dictated from the runways. Clichéd as it may sound, we are still trying to "have it all," while reinventing ourselves in the process.

GOLD HULA GIRL CHARMS. (TRACEY ZABAR)

AN EXTRAORDINARY GOLD BRACELET. CHARMS INCLUDE A LARGE IVORY OPERA PASS. ELIZABETH TAYLOR INHERITED A NECKLACE FROM EDITH HEAD WITH THIRTEEN OF THESE IVORY THEATRE PASSES. (KIM, KATHLEEN, KENDALL, AND LINDSEY BARRETT)

famous CHARMERS

I HAVE LOVED

NOTORIOUS LOVE AFFAIRS, GENEROUS CIRCLES OF ILLUSTRIOUS FRIENDS, STELLAR ACHIEVEMENTS, AND ONE-OF-A-KIND PERSONALITIES—THIS IS THE STUFF OF WHICH LEGENDARY CHARM BRACELETS ARE MADE. LOOK TO THESE EMINENT LADIES OF STYLE FOR SOME CHARM BRACELET INSPIRATION.

THE BALL-ARNAZ FAMILY

FACT ONE: THE CHARM BRACELET SERVED AS THE ARCHETYPAL ACCESSORY OF THE 1950S.

A VERY SPECIAL BRACELET FOR GRACE, THE OWNER'S DAUGHTER, FEATURING: A TIBETAN SYMBOL FOR INNER PEACE; TWO HAND-ENGRAVED SMILEY FACES FROM 1948; A TOILET THAT ONCE FLEW OFF THE BRACELET AND PINGED A PRICELESS MING VASE; AND A ST. CHRISTOPHER MEDAL CARRIED BY THE OWNER'S FATHER-IN-LAW ON FLIGHTS DURING WORLD WAR II. THERE WAS ONCE AN ENVELOPE CHARM ON THIS BRACELET WITH A LETTER INSIDE THAT WAS ENGRAVED "BEST FRIENDS FOREVER." THIS CHARM, AND THE FRIEND, ARE GONE FOREVER. (ALEXANDRA TROWER LINDSEY)

FACT TWO: The most famous poster girl of the 1950s was the lovable Lucille Ball. Put the two together and what do you get?

FACT THREE: Charm bracelets were near and dear to the Ball-Arnaz family's heart. Both Lucy and Desi's mothers wore charm bracelets all the time. Lucy herself wore a prized gold bracelet celebrating the musical career of husband Desi, who had it made for her as a surprise; the charms were six records, each engraved with one of his hit songs on the A and B sides. Lucy and Desi created an adorable bracelet for daughter Lucie, as well. Little Lucie's bracelet has a grand piano that opens, a wishing well, a whistle that works, a ballerina, a carousel pony, an enameled clown, a lavishly decorated birthday cake, and a frying pan with an enameled fried egg. Lucie Arnaz also has a lovely gold bracelet from her youth with various medals and charms of saints, a gold coin, a cross, a heart engraved with the misspelled LUCY, and another heart engraved HAZEL (both were a birthday gift from a woman named Hazel who was Lucille Ball's stand-in on the *I Love Lucy* show), and a charm engraved LUCIE DESIREE ARNAZ.

Desi Arnaz must have taken

TOP AND BOTTOM: TWO CHILDHOOD BRACELETS. (LUCIE ARNAZ)

BRACELET OWNED BY LUCILLE BALL. (LUCIE ARNAZ)

great delight in a charm necklace he added to as Lucie was growing up: A heart from 1959 says "Love, Daddy" and is accompanied by a separate key, and a 1963 calendar has Lucie's birthday marked with a ruby. Lucie's husband, Larry Luckinbill, continued the family tradition and bestowed upon his wife a bracelet with a trumpet charm symbolizing a show she once did, a top hat and cane for her dancing, and a heart made of rubies, her birthstone.

LILLY DACHÉ

Legendary milliner Lilly Daché knew a thing or two about glamour. So much so that she wrote a book on it (*Lilly Daché's Glamour Book,* published in 1956). And in between making amazing chapeaux, writing books, running a successful costume jewelry and cosmetics company, and taking a young designer named Halston under her wing, the unstoppable Ms. Daché tossed around bon mots with ease. "There is no such thing as luck. We make our own, good or bad," she said. How would she explain, then, the charming Philippe Halsman photograph of her from the 1940s, where she is dripping in coin charm bracelets (much like her style sisters, Elsa Schiaparelli and Coco Chanel), with one charm that features a "lucky" 13?

☙ A FINE GOLD BRACELET WITH WHIMSICAL CHARMS. (KIM BARRETT)

☙ A LOVELY GOLD BANGLE SUSPENDED WITH SEVEN NINETEENTH-CENTURY GOLD BRITISH COINS. THE ENGRAVING ON ONE SIDE OF EACH COIN WAS POLISHED OFF, AND A NAME OR MONOGRAM WAS RE-ENGRAVED. (ANONYMOUS)

Friends and lovers are swell, but when it comes to charm bracelets, you can always count on yourself to get what you want. Sultry screen actress Arlene Dahl, mother of Lorenzo Lamas, has five meaningful charms on her gold bracelet. Two of the charms were gifts from herself (a gold sun for her August birth month and a gold and pearl Norwegian tree of life in honor of her heritage), two were gifts from husbands (a red ruby and diamond heart from Fernando Lamas to mark their first wedding anniversary, and a gold dahlia from her current husband, Marc Rosen, to celebrate the 1976 launch of her first fragrance, the somewhat eponymous "Dahlia"), and one was a gift from a costar (a green enamel four-leaf clover with a diamond in the center from actor Dennis Morgan on the occasion of her film debut in *My Wild Irish Rose*). Ms. Dahl copied her bracelet for her jewelry business.

A good charm bracelet can reflect both the highs and lows of a life, and in effect become a personal talisman. The brilliant, multitalented Phyllis Diller is the owner of one such magical bracelet, which she wore constantly in the 1960s. Each charm represented her dreams and the things she wanted to do and make happen. Some of the charms were gifts; others she bought herself. I had the pleasure of having Miss Diller talk me through each one:

1. A martini shaker with a tiny red devil inside—"I'm a martini person, and after a couple of martinis, the devil comes out."

2. A gold charm of the Waldorf-Astoria Hotel, a place Miss Diller loved to stay.

3. The skyline of New York.

4. An old-fashioned microphone, because she did many interviews in the days of radio.

5. A little gold box holding the "tiniest *New York Times*" to commemorate her first writing she was really proud of, which was published in the *Times Magazine*.

6. An oil well, because she always wanted to own oil.

7. An old-fashioned cash register: "I was always interested in making money."

8. A flattened penny that her son put on a railroad track many years ago, with a prayer engraved on it.

9. A gold movie camera.

10. "Now, there's a fun one, not solid gold. It's really a paper clip." Miss Diller was hurt by a bad business deal, and the paper clip reminds her to "be careful, and don't sign contracts."

11. The next one tells a poignant story. "I was honored by a Pittsburgh organization as their Woman of the Year. Pittsburgh had a

THESE TWO BRACELETS ARE ALWAYS WORN TOGETHER BY A FABULOUS 86-YEAR-OLD WOMAN. HER FELLOW STUDENTS AT HARVARD (WHICH SHE HAS BEEN ATTENDING SINCE 1982) ASKED HER TO PLEASE NOT WEAR SUCH NOISY BRACELETS. RATHER THAN TAKE THEM OFF, SHE COVERED THEM WITH A TERRY-CLOTH SWEAT BAND DURING CLASS. (JANE WELT)

for each month

BIRTHSTONES, FLOWERS OF THE MONTHS, AND BIRTH WISHES

Month	Birthstone	Flower	Birth Wish
JANUARY:	Garnet	Carnation	Loyalty
FEBRUARY:	Amethyst	Violet	Sincerity
MARCH:	Aquamarine	Daffodil	Courage
APRIL:	Diamond	Sweet Pea	Purity
MAY:	Emerald	Lily of the Valley	Happiness
JUNE:	Pearl	Rose	Intuition
JULY:	Ruby	Larkspur	Love
AUGUST:	Peridot	Gladiolus	Peace
SEPTEMBER:	Sapphire	Aster	Wisdom
OCTOBER:	Opal	Marigold	Hope
NOVEMBER:	Topaz	Chrysanthemum	Knowledge
DECEMBER:	Turquoise	Narcissus	Success

A PERFECT PERSONAL CHARM BRACELET IN GOLD, WITH BRA, PANTIES, DIAMOND ENGAGEMENT RING, TINTYPE PICTURE, AND ICE CREAM CART CHARMS. (TRACEY ZABAR)

stadium with a retractable roof. It was interesting architecturally." Miss Diller put the stadium charm on her bracelet because she dreamed at that luncheon of one day playing somewhere that grand. Sure enough, much later, she played her first symphony date as a concert pianist at that very same stadium. At the time she said, "All my dreams have come true."

12. A ruby birthstone charm, in honor of her daughter.

13. "One of my records."

14. A disc jockey in Australia gave her a little gold kangaroo.

15. A sister-in-law gave her a charm with an eight-million-year-old stone from Petoskey, Michigan.

16. A gold Water Tower Inn charm, from a hotel in Chicago, is next. "I loved it so much."

17. "A gold television, with a teeny tiny 'my' face inside."

18. The next two charms are comedy and tragedy charms that light up.

19. "Jack Paar gave me a gold British coin with Elizabeth II on it."

We talked about what to do with a piece of jewelry that you love. "What am I going to do with this?" Miss Diller asked me. I said, "Miss Diller, you have grandchildren, don't you?" "Yes, four grandsons." Since I have four sons, we commiserated about boys' lack of interest in jewelry. She told me, "Boys are easier, but all you can give them is a shovel." Well said.

MRS. WALT DISNEY

When you win an Oscar, it's something to write home about. When you manage to bag twenty-two of 'em, why not announce your achievements to everyone in town and buy your wife a charm bracelet full of adorable miniature gold men? Walt Disney did just that for his wife—her unique bracelet displayed one scaled-down Oscar for each of the real ones he won between 1931 and 1964.

A GOOFY CARTOON CHARACTER BRACELET DATING FROM THE 1970S AND 1980S. (TRACEY ZABAR)

A WHIMSICAL LITTLE BRACELET OF FINE GOLD, ENAMEL, AND STONE, WHICH WAS MADE FROM THE LATE 1950S TO THE EARLY 1960S FOR A YOUNG GIRL. THE BIRTHDAY CAKE WAS ONCE COVERED IN PINK ENAMEL ICING, AND THE EXTREMELY RARE AQUARIUM HAS TWO GOLD FISH WHICH TREMBLE BEHIND GREEN GLASS. (CAROL HOCHMAN)

pardon my french

As languages go, French is pretty charming in and of itself. Engrave something in French on a charm, and suddenly a sentiment is all the more endearing.

Qu'hier que demain. (I love you more today than yesterday), but less than tomorrow.

Comment est-ce que je t'aime? Laisse-moi compter les façons. How do I love thee? Let me count the ways.

Séparés mais toujours unis. Separated but always together.

Le temps est plus precieux depuis que je vous aime. Time is more precious since I have you to love.

Merci mille fois pour mille choses. A thousand thanks for a thousand things.

On a roulette wheel from 1958: *Je t'aime...un peu...beaucoup ...passion...à la folie...pas du tout....* I love you...a little...very much ...passionately...with madness ...not at all....

cultural charms

CHINESE CHARMS: Buddhas, jade carvings, Chinese symbols for good luck, "double happiness," and prosperity

FABERGÉ EGGS: Enameled eggs from the celebrated jeweler Fabergé made popular in the court of Czar Nicholas II and worn in miniature on a bracelet by the Czarina Alexandra; eggs have long symbolized life, hope, prosperity, and renewal in Russian culture

IRISH CHARMS: The four-leaf clover, the claddagh, the Celtic love knot

MILAGROS: Latin American and Italian flat charms in the shapes of body parts and animal amulets; used at shrines to petition the saints for health and prosperity

NETSUKE: Small toggles that hung from cords to keep silk pouches closed on Japanese kimonos; often carved into whimsical objects and made of ivory, wood, gemstones, coral, and shells

Those pillbox hats! Those big-lens sunglasses! Jacqueline Bouvier Kennedy Onassis remains a powerful force in our collective American fashion memory as an arbiter of unquestionable taste. Did Jackie wear charm bracelets? Sure, but she did it her own unmistakable way. She was occasionally photographed wearing bracelets that made a singular statement with just one large charm. It is, of course, a look that will never go out of style, just like the lady herself. She also owned a gold link bracelet with twenty-five charms, which was sold at the Sotheby's auction of her belongings in 1996.

Interestingly, President Kennedy himself seems to have had a penchant for these sentimental baubles. In the very same desk where his son was so famously photographed poking his head out of a little door on the bottom, there was a special drawer where he is said to have kept personal mementos of great importance. Two of the items were charm bracelets! One was an Irish-themed bracelet, perhaps a souvenir of his trip to his ancestral home or a gift from a relative. It had a shamrock, a horseshoe, and charms spelling out J F KENNEDY, and was sold at auction for a whopping $32,000 plus. The other bracelet had one charm, a horse's head; on the reverse, MACARONI—the name of Caroline Kennedy's pony—was engraved. The links of this bracelet were letters spelling out the name CAROLINE. It is unknown whether these bracelets were the President's lucky charms, if they belonged to his daughter, or if they were intended as gifts.

For those regular folk looking to don a little of the magic of Kennedy Camelot, there were multitudes of Kennedy-themed charm bracelets available as souvenirs or giveaways from the 1960

☞ A LARGE GOLD BRACELET. THE HEART CHARM WITH A BASKET OF GEMSTONE FLOWERS IS TYPICAL OF THE LATE 1950S AND EARLY 1960S. THIS FAMILY CONTINUES THE TRADITION OF PASSING ON A CHARM BRACELET TO EACH GIRL TO MARK HER SIXTEENTH BIRTHDAY. (NAN MUTNICK)

☞ A WONDERFUL CHARM BRACELET, WITH NATURAL PEARLS SET WITH PINK SAPPHIRES AND MANY DIFFERENT COLORS OF GOLD. CHARMS INCLUDE A RABBIT WITH A DIAMOND COLLAR, A HUNTING DOG, A SWAN, A ROOSTER, AND A HAND WITH EMERALDS AND DIAMONDS. POSSIBLY RUSSIAN, IT IS FROM THE EARLY 1900S. (FRED LEIGHTON)

presidential campaign. One example had four charms with real photographs of President Kennedy, Mrs. Kennedy, Caroline, and John, Jr. Others had the names of the four family members written in script or little busts of their heads. One bracelet featured a PT 109 boat; an eternal flame torch; a scroll worded with the President's famous call to "Ask not what your country can do for you, ask what you can do for your country"; and a rocking chair.

GINGER ROGERS

Fred Astaire's favorite leading lady owned a bracelet as graceful and feminine as her dance moves. Sold at auction in 1996 by Christie's in Los Angeles, the platinum rectangular-link bracelet featured five lovely charms: a white enamel and diamond "I love you" telephone; an enamel, cultured pearl, and diamond bouquet of flowers; a platinum and diamond ring; a platinum and diamond eternity band; and a platinum and diamond music staff.

MRS. BABE RUTH

Sometimes, in lieu of her own achievements, a woman's charm bracelet documented those of her husband. Babe Ruth was larger than life, and his career with the New York Yankees is one of the most unforgettable in sports history. Mrs. Ruth's fourteen-karat gold bracelet held seven charms that were a testament to the Bambino's love and mastery of the game: a baseball bat, a cap with 1927 engraved on the brim for the year Babe hit his record sixtieth home

A MAGNIFICENT GOLD BRACELET WITH CHARMS COLLECTED BY JOAN GOLDBERG SARNOFF. (SUSAN SARNOFF BRAM)

THIS AMUSING BRACELET CELEBRATES TWENTY-FOUR YEARS OF MARRIAGE, WITH CHARMS OF GOLD, ENAMEL, DIAMONDS, PEARLS, AND GEMS. OF NOTE ARE PERIOD CHARMS SUCH AS REVERSE-PAINTED CRYSTAL INTAGLIOS, HAIR LOCKETS, AND A PORTRAIT OF KING EDWARD VII AND QUEEN ALEXANDRA, CIRCA 1905. (TRACEY ZABAR)

run, a ball engraved 60 to commemorate the same, a shoe with cleats, a base, a batting figure with 3 engraved on the back of his uniform (Babe's number, now of course retired), and a rectangular charm with a baseball coat of arms—a pair of crossed bats and a ball with the Yankees logo in relief—on one side and her name engraved on the other. The bracelet was auctioned in 1999 at Sotheby's in New York; it sold for nearly fourteen times the amount of the estimate of the sale.

MRS. PAUL WHITEMAN

Taking the maxim of getting by with a little help from your friends to envious new levels, the wife of the famous bandleader, the self-styled "King of Jazz," who led the most popular dance band of the 1920s, amassed an amazing assortment of charms and applied them to a pair of wide, hinged cuff bracelets in fourteen-karat pink gold. The Whitemans' astounding roster of friends who contributed to the bracelets from the late 1930s through the 1950s reads like a who's who of charmers from days gone by: Louis Armstrong, Charlie Chaplin, Maurice Chevalier, Bing Crosby, Walt Disney, Douglas Fairbanks, Sr., F. Scott Fitzgerald, Henry Ford, Bob Hope, Buster Keaton, Joseph Kennedy, Charles Lindbergh, and the Duke of Windsor. The various charms were embellished with diamonds, cabochon and calibré-cut stones, and enamel. These extraordinary bangles were sold at auction by Sotheby's in 1995.

TOP: THIS BRACELET IS HAND CRAFTED OF EIGHTEEN-KARAT GOLD, WITH THIRTEEN SHELLS OF VARYING COLORS OF NATURAL CORAL. EACH SHELL HAS TWISTS OF GOLD, DRIPPING DIAMONDS ON THE SHELLS. (MISH) BOTTOM: MRS. PAUL WHITEMAN'S CHARM BRACELETS. (SOTHEBY'S)

DIAMOND AND ONYX CHARM BRACELET. (CHRISTIE'S)

THE DUCHESS OF WINDSOR

Not only did this American-born divorcée get a noble title and her guy (Edward, who gave up being king of England to become the Duke of Windsor so he could take her as his wife), but the achingly chic Wallis Simpson also got her hands on perhaps the most famous charm bracelet of all time. Made by Cartier in the 1930s, the platinum bracelet was dripping with gem-encrusted and gold crosses. Each cross was inscribed with a memory of one of the moments of the duo's life together. Other royals who owned charm bracelets were Princess Grace and Diana, Princess of Wales.

MRS. HARRY WINSTON

If you happen to be the wife of one of the world's most famous jewelers, your own baubles should speak volumes. Mrs. Winston's fabulous charm bracelet didn't disappoint. With links crafted in white gold and cultured pearls, the bracelet exhibited an impressive array of twenty-three different charms mounted in gold, silver, and platinum and decorated with diamonds, colored gems, and enamel. Included were many animals, hearts, a baby carriage, a wheelbarrow, and a jack-in-the-box with the devil's head (one can only wonder about the meaning of that last one). The bracelet was sold at auction in 1992 by Sotheby's in New York.

DEBBIE REYNOLDS

The actress has a very tiny sterling silver charm bracelet, which she received as a gift when she was a young girl. She described it as decorated with Asian motifs, including a pagoda, a water bucket, a Chinese figure, a Buddha, a fish, bells, a teahouse, and a junk (boat).

CONNIE STEVENS

Funnyman Jerry Lewis gave Ms. Stevens a delightful charm bracelet.

DEBRA WINGER

The actress' mother cut up her charm bracelet and gave her children their respective engraved charms commemorating their births.

NATALIE WOOD

The young actress—usually in the company of future husband Robert Wagner—was often photographed for 1950s fanzines and promotional stills wearing assorted charm bracelets.

CHARMED TALES I'VE BEEN TOLD

For as long as I've been wearing charm bracelets, people have shared personal stories with me about bracelets they have known. I've heard fond reminiscences and funny recollections, as well as heart-wrenching tales of jewels lost and stolen. It's an emotional topic. Women have wept when telling me of the experience of collecting charms through the moments of their lives. Unforgettable memories poured out—helping Mother dress for a social engagement, the scent of her perfume wafting through the air, the thrilling ritual of climbing on a

A DELIGHTFUL GOLD CHARM BRACELET FROM THE 1940S WITH UNIQUE CHARMS, INCLUDING TWO LARGE FOUR-LEAF CLOVERS ENGRAVED WITH INITIALS AND DATES, A HUGE POODLE IN A HOOP, AND A MOON CHARM WITH PEARLS. ONE CHARM IS ENGRAVED "50, EH? WELL, WE LOVE YOU ANYWAY! BLONDE AND BLACKHEAD." (ANONYMOUS)

chair to remove the sacred charm bracelet box from the closet shelf while a little sister jealously looks on. Stories like these continue to captivate me and fuel my passion for charm bracelets even more:

○ A man told of a competition between his aunts when he was a boy to create the "fullest charm bracelet ever," which ultimately had to evolve into the "great charm necklace competition" once they ran out of links on their bracelets. He and all the other children were quick to behave when they heard those noisy things coming around the corner.

○ My aunt Devon told of a childhood trip alone on a plane, during which a lady from Texas kept her entertained all the way to London with tales of each of the charms on her bracelet.

○ In honor of putting up with a somewhat difficult husband for all those years, a grandmother received a Purple Heart charm on a bracelet for her fortieth anniversary. She countered with the fact that it hadn't really been so bad, and in fact she felt she'd had a wonderful life full of love, attention, and luxuries. Upon second thought, she then added that she indeed deserved it because she had "never had a headache" throughout their entire relationship, if you know what I mean.

○ Throughout World War II, a couple in Europe presented their beloved daughter with charms they had collected before war broke out. Although this family had terrible deprivations, they wanted their little girl to feel special and still have some joys in life during hard times. Today, the little handmade gold animal charms are on a bracelet the owner and her daughter each take turns wearing.

A GOLD BRACELET FROM THE 1950S WITH TEN EXTREMELY LARGE CHARMS, INCLUDING A DISK WITH A SILHOUETTE OF A GIRL ON ONE SIDE AND A DAUGHTER'S NAME ENGRAVED ON THE REVERSE, AND ANOTHER DISK WITH A SILHOUETTE OF A BOY ON THE FRONT AND FOUR SONS' NAMES ENGRAVED ON THE REVERSE. (GRACE COLANGELO)

And from the unfortunate "gone but not forgotten" department:

○ A dear friend, whom I had known for years, casually mentioned her mother's charm bracelet when she was admiring mine. I asked where it was, and she said that it was lost in the war. War? What war? It seemed that her father was an ambassador when the family had to flee the country during a revolution. All their personal belongings, including the charm bracelet, were left behind and lost forever.

○ An artist friend told me that she had to make herself a charm bracelet because as a child she was obsessed with a marvelous one full of charms that was worn by her favorite aunt. The uncle was rumored to have been in the Mob. Over the years, the family fell on tough times and the bracelet mysteriously disappeared.

○ A woman told me that as a young girl in the 1950s she returned home from junior high school one day to find her mother had thrown out her charm collection. Like a boy who had his precious comic book and baseball card collections tossed by Mom, she never quite got over this. She is now an antique jewelry dealer.

○ A heartbroken former New York City Ballet dancer relayed how she collected charms for her bracelet wherever the company toured around the globe. Her bracelet was stolen long ago, but she still recalls its bear from Bern, Switzerland; two Lipizzaner horses from Vienna; Mozart's bust from the Salzburg Festival; a shark from Australia; chopsticks and a kimono complete with a red enamel obi from Japan; and of course, ballet shoes and a ballerina.

GREEN CELLULOID BRACELET WITH BAKELITE CHARM. (TRACEY ZABAR)

CHAPTER
3

charm SCHOOL

BUT ENOUGH OF ALL THE THEORIZING AND REMINISCING. LET'S GET ON TO THE GOOD STUFF, LIKE HOW DO YOU GO ABOUT GETTING YOUR HANDS ON A CHARM BRACELET OF YOUR OWN?

COMPOSING YOUR OWN CHARM BRACELET

FIRST, DECIDE WHICH SIDE OF THE FENCE YOU ARE ON: DO-IT-YOUR-SELF OR PREFAB. ARE YOU THE TYPE OF CHARM BRACELETER WHO ENJOYS THE THRILL OF THE HUNT AND COLLECTS CHARM MEMENTOS OVER TIME? OR ARE YOU THE INSTANT-GRATIFICATION TYPE WHO SEES A GORGEOUS READY-MADE BRACELET THAT STOPS YOU DEAD IN YOUR TRACKS AND THAT YOU MUST HAVE IMMEDIATELY? OF COURSE, EITHER

AREN'T MY CHILDREN CHARMING? (JANICE CEGIELSKI)

THE ULTIMATE SILVER BRACELET ASSEMBLED WITH CHARMS COLLECTED FROM 1964 TO THE PRESENT. THE MANY PERIOD CHARMS ARE SET WITH RUBIES, SAP-PHIRES, EMERALDS, RHODOLITE GARNETS, AND PEARLS. (TRACEY ZABAR)

way is totally acceptable! If you decide to collect charms over time, you'll need a bracelet.

Now you need to commit to a metal. Do you want a gold charm bracelet or a silver one? Gold is much more valuable and expensive. Silver is more casual and often a more appropriate choice for a young girl. However, don't assume that silver is much cheaper than gold—the labor involved in handmade jewelry is expensive for all metals. Inasmuch as you can, always opt for real gold and sterling silver. Although higher-karat gold is usually the rule for finer jewelry, stick to fourteen karat for charm bracelets. It will stand up to the clinging and clanging of the charms. Eighteen karat is just too soft; it gets very dinged up. If you have a beautiful charm of eighteen-karat gold or higher, ignore what I just said, and put it on your bracelet. Many charms of the fifties were made of base metal or were gold-filled; avoid them, unless there is great sentiment attached. They look cheap, and there is a fine line between funky and cheesy. Many British charms were often nine karat; this is fine, and the color can be quite nice. Now, if money is no object and you live for jewelry, you can even go for platinum. But in general, buy what you will love and wear.

Also, think stylistically about the charms themselves—do you prefer highbrow gems (i. e., a diamond-encrusted heart) or inside jokes (i. e., a sterling silver scale for when you finally shed those ten pesky pounds)? Consider color. If you'd like to add a splash of color with enamel, gems, or different golds to enliven a basic metal bracelet, add lots. A gold bracelet with one colored charm doesn't make sense. Remember, sometimes more is more. Use real stones and pearls as often as possible. Since most of the stones are tiny, they aren't that expensive. You don't need the most perfect color or

TOP: THE PROUD MAMA OF A HARVARD MAN ASSEMBLED THIS GOLD BRACELET FROM HER SON'S SPORTING AWARDS AND LATER GAVE IT TO HER DAUGHTER-IN-LAW. (LOUISE LIPSEY HARPEL) CENTER: THE SISTER BRACELET TO ONE WORN BY THE CHARACTER CARRIE BRADSHAW IN A NUMBER OF EPISODES OF *SEX AND THE CITY*. (TRACEY ZABAR) BOTTOM: WONDERFUL ENGRAVED BABY BOOTIES IN ROSE GOLD SUSPENDED FROM A MATCHING WATCH CHAIN WITH SWIVEL CLASP. (TRACEY ZABAR)

charm types

CONTAINER CHARMS: Designed to hold something within, say, a little pillbox or perfume bottle, or some type of container for a baby tooth, a lock of hair, a pinch of sand. A locket is a variation on this.

DOCUMENT CHARMS: Engravable charms like birth or marriage certificates, driver's licenses, diplomas, birth dates on calendars, or messages.

FIGURAL/3-D CHARMS: Probably the most popular and widely available. You'll find everything from animals to buildings to people to everyday objects.

MECHANICAL CHARMS: Charms that have some element that moves—for example, candles that pop up on a birthday cake when you press a little lever, or a tiny "love-o-meter" with a movable arrow that points to "yes," "no," or "maybe." There are also miniature music box charms that really work. A variation on this is the spinner charm, usually a little disc with letters strategically placed on each side; when the disc is spun, an optical illusion is created and you can read a secret message such as "I love you."

SILHOUETTE/FLAT CHARMS: Pretty self-explanatory. States, children's heads, shields, nautical or semaphore flags, initials, and coins are all common examples.

STANHOPE CHARMS: These vintage charms usually have a little peephole covered in a magnifying glass. On the inside you can see a minuscule series of words or images, often a prayer, the Constitution, or scenes of a place like San Francisco etched or painted on glass. Many Stanhopes are damaged, as the glass that the scenes are etched on is often shattered or crazed, or the magnifying peep is missing.

A DELIGHTFUL COLLECTION OF CHARMS, INCLUDING CAMEOS, ENAMELED SAINTS, AND PAVÉ CHARMS WITH PRECIOUS STONES AND PEARLS. (ROBIN DEUTSCH)

quality; just make sure that the stones are pretty and that you don't see any obvious inclusions or chips.

Next, determine what type of composition you would like. You can have a charm bracelet with one lone charm, huge or tiny. Or you can have a few strategically placed charms to make a medium-sized bracelet where each charm pops. These require a bit of rhythm and editing to look right, and odd numbers tend to look best (though avoid the number thirteen, unless you think it's lucky). At the other end of the spectrum, you can pile charms on ad infinitum. These dripping ones require less order—the more, the merrier. It helps to hang one charm, usually the heaviest, opposite the clasp, so gravity works in your favor. The clasp stays on top, and your charm bracelet is always perfectly positioned on your wrist.

If you are going the collecting route, you might want to consider buying charms in just one category—dogs, hearts, buildings, or flower charms, for example. It is easier to ask each jewelry dealer at an antiques show, "Do you carry gold hula girl charms?" than to have to pick through every box of charms at each booth. Some collectors wear a sign on a baseball cap saying "looking to buy silver elephant charms." I'm not such a fan of rats, snakes, and spiders, but if you

find that you love them, by all means put them on your bracelet. The only charm I ever feel is forbidden is anything X-rated. Little kids adore looking at charm bracelets... enough said.

The more specific you are, and the narrower your collection, the quicker your flea market trips will be. You might even get lucky and find a dealer who specializes in your area of interest. I have a relationship with a picker (these people generally act as a middle person between the seller of an item and a dealer and may be on the lookout for certain items for different customers) from Europe who has the most amazing taste. I always try to buy her whole bag o' charms. Alternatively, you may wish to build a bracelet by theme, say cooking or the four seasons. Or you may simply choose to have a hodgepodge of charms that represent things that are special to you. The bracelets are meant to be charming and humorous and, above all, to reflect who you are and what you love.

For a personal note, consider having a little charm engraved in your grandparents' native language. Chinese and Hebrew look quite lovely. There is a gorgeousness to hand engraving. Always try to splurge for it.

A WONDERFUL, UNUSUAL CAMERA CHARM BRACELET COLLECTED OVER MANY YEARS BY TWO ANTIQUE CAMERA BUFFS, JERRY AND SHIRLEY SPRUNG. THE PINK AND YELLOW GOLD AND STERLING SILVER BRACELET WAS INHERITED BY THEIR DAUGHTER. (SARA SPRUNG)

DON'T FORGET MY BIRTHDAY. A STERLING SILVER CHARM BRACELET, WITH ROUND DISKS HAND ENGRAVED IN A LOVELY SCRIPT. THERE ARE SIX CHARMS, EACH WITH A CHILD'S NAME ON THE FRONT AND A BIRTH DATE ON THE REVERSE. (TRACEY ZABAR)

RULES TO LIVE BY

Building a charm bracelet can quickly become an addictive, all-consuming passion. Try to control yourself somewhat. Buy what you love, not what you just like a little. If you overbuy, what are you going to do with the extra charms? You can give them away or trade them, but unless you are going to go into business and become a dealer, think about the clutter of one more collection. If you have overbought, all is not lost; check out the Beyond the Bracelet ideas chapter.

Educate yourself in the market. If this is going to be your next magnificent obsession, look around first before you buy. You will be very annoyed if you overpay for a charm. That said, if you see an unusual or antique charm that you adore, "get it or you'll regret it"—even if you are overpaying. You might never see that particular charm again, and we all remember the ones that got away.

One word regarding copyrights: Most charms are designed to be sold as separate components to be added one at a time to a bracelet. It is reasonable to use charms on a bracelet that you are composing yourself. However, do not attempt to copy charms. Making molds and recasting them is a no-no, so don't do it.

charm bracelet themes

I'm torn. Lord knows I'm a sucker for a well-stocked bracelet with a hodgepodge of charms from nearly every minute of the wearer's life. What's great about these bracelets is their breaking of the rules and the constant surprise of the different charms you find dangling from them. That said, some of my favorite bracelets have had very specific themes. Themed charms can be a lot of fun to collect, and with thousands upon thousands of charms out there, it can help to know what you're looking for. Here are a few ideas to inspire you.

FOR THE TRAVELER: Paris, London, Italy, New York, Miami, Cuba, Hawaii, Egypt, South of the Border, United States, Beach Vacations, Landmarks, Gourmet, Art, Transportation, Maps, the World's Fair, Buddhas, Around the World

FOR THE FASHIONISTA: Shoes, Pocketbooks, Makeup, Undies, Earrings, Mink Coats, Dresses, Hats, Hair, Beauty

FOR THE ROMANTIC: Hearts, Cupids, Angels, Devils, Love, Valentine, I Love You, Engagement, Honeymoon, the Secret Language of Flowers, Clocks, the Four Seasons

FOR THE SENTIMENTAL: Let It Snow, Take Me Out to the Ball Game, Sweetheart, Religious, Hands, Jewels, Initials, Words, Lockets, Moons and Stars, Photos, I Remember You, Best Friends, Millennium, Milagros, Anniversary, Happy New Year, Easter Eggs, Merry Christmas, the Twelve Days of Christmas, Happy Hanukkah, Kwanzaa

FOR THE LUCKY CHARMER: Las Vegas, Monaco, Gambling, Four-leaf Clover, Coins, Poker Chips, Good Luck, Dice, Playing Cards, Roulette Wheel, One-armed Bandit, Money, Mechanicals that Move, Stanhopes that Have Peepholes, Chess Pieces, Halloween, Horseshoes, Zodiac

A CHANEL CHARM BRACELET. (TRACEY ZABAR)

IN A WHIMSICAL NOD TO THE OWNER'S LAST NAME, THIS WONDERFUL GOLD BRACELET HAS MULTIPLE CHARMS DEPICTING THE MOON. (NANCY MOON)

more charm bracelet themes

FOR THE MOVIE STAR: Hollywood, Broadway, Chorus Girl, A Star is Born, This is Your Life, Theater, Television, Movies

FOR THE ANIMAL LOVER: Elephants, Donkeys, Monkeys, Cats, Kittens, Puppies, Dogs, Horses, Butterflies, Birds, Pigs, Safari, Dinosaurs, Endangered Species, Bunnies, Poodles

FOR THE LITTLE GIRL: First Day of School, the Years of Your Life, Teddy Bears, My Childhood, Cartoon Characters, Toys, Snoopy, Sports, Camp, Brownies, Girl Scouts, Dance, Ballet, School Days, Cowgirl, Birthstone, Circus, Little Miss, Campfire Girl

FOR THE BIG GIRL: First Date, Teenager, Girlfriends, Sweet 16, Bat Mitzvah, Equestrian, Teenybopper, Record Albums, Elvis, the Beatles, the Monkees, High School, Bobby Soxer, College, Spring Break, Sorority Sister, Graduation, Frank Sinatra, Liberace, Feminist, I Quit Smoking, Alcoholic, Overeater

FOR THE CAREER GIRL: First Job, Secretary, Stewardess, Nurse, Teacher, Astronaut, Medical, Dental, Military, Lawyer, Hippie, Gardener, Musical Instruments

FOR THE BRIDE: Will You Marry Me?, Engagement, Bridal Shower, Bridesmaid, Bride and Groom, Houses, Household Appliances, the Perfect Husband, Anniversary

FOR THE MUM: Babies, New Mother, Baby Shower, Children of the Week, My Family's Birthdays, Grandmother

A STERLING SILVER BRACELET WITH CHARMS COLLECTED OVER A NUMBER OF YEARS AT CAMP STRAWDERMAN IN THE SHENANDOAH MOUNTAINS. THE CHARMS INCLUDE A PIXIE FOR TUMBLING, A PADDLEBOAT FOR PERFORMING IN *SHOWBOAT,* TROPHIES, AND CABINS, PLUS AWARDS FOR SWIMMING, ARCHERY, CAMP SPIRIT, AND BEING AN "OLD GIRL." (SUSAN MORGENTHAU)

THE DOGS OF MY LIFE. FINE GOLD DOG CHARMS, INCLUDING A COLLIE, COCKER SPANIEL, BEDLINGTON TERRIER, DALMATIAN, PEKINGESE, AND CORGI. OTHER CHARMS ARE REVERSE-PAINTED GLASS INTAGLIOS SET INTO GOLD, PLUS A FINE ENAMELED HOUND. (TRACEY ZABAR)

Quirky British clothing designer Paul Smith observed: "You can find inspiration in everything …and if you can't, look again." I recommend you get in touch with your inner gatherer and take the same approach to charm hunting. And don't underestimate what you might already have right under your nose: twee bits in your jewelry box, every little thing your aunt pressed into your hand when you were a girl because you oh so loved gold, a gorgeous earring without a mate, and the pendant you adore that doesn't quite look right on a necklace. Old rings, baby rings, and sorority pins often look sweet on a bracelet when mixed with everything else. Beyond that, here are some of my favorite common and not so common places to find charms new and old.

SHOPS AND SALES

Antique shops, consignment shops, resale shops, junk shops, thrift stores, jewelry stores, museum shops, pawnshops, department stores, toy stores, church bazaars, dollhouse shops, craft stores, charity auctions, garage sales, yard sales

WORLDWIDE FLEA MARKETS

LONDON: Portobello Road, Camden Passage, Covent Garden, Gray's Antique Markets PARIS: Marché aux Puces de Vanves, Marché aux Puces de Saint-Ouen/Clignancourt

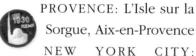

PROVENCE: L'Isle sur la Sorgue, Aix-en-Provence NEW YORK CITY: Twenty-sixth Street Flea Market MASSACHUSETTS: Brimfield Antique Show

CALIFORNIA: Pasadena Rose Bowl Swap Meet

AUCTION HOUSES

Christie's, Sotheby's, William Doyle Galleries, Bonhams & Butterfields, Skinner, Dupuis

ONLINE

Ebay, search engines, jewelry web sites, charm enthusiast sites (for swapping)

WHEREVER

On vacation, in your junk drawer, in your jewelry box, in your mother's jewelry box, in your sister's jewelry box, among your child's collection of flotsam and Monopoly pieces, through trades with friends and other collectors, just about everywhere

A COLLECTION OF GIRLY CHARMS. (TRACEY ZABAR)

72

the secret language of flowers

In matters of love and friendship, the poor Victorians could never just say what they meant. Instead they lived by an intricate system of cryptic codes and symbols. Even flowers weren't safe from their clandestine communications; the Victorians assigned a hidden meaning to each flower known as the "Secret Language of Flowers." Today, this "secret language" adds another layer of meaning to flower charms on a bracelet.

Angelica: Inspiration
Baby's Breath: Everlasting Love
Bluebell: Constancy
Buttercup: Cheerfulness
Daffodil: Respect
Daisy: Innocence
Fern: Sincerity
Forget Me Not: True Love
Heather: Admiration
Holly: Happiness
Hyacinth: Play
Iris: Faith
Ivy: Friendship
Jasmine: Amiability
Lavender: Devotion
Lily: Beauty

Lily of the Valley: Sweetness
Magnolia: Nobility
Marigold: Comfort
Myrtle: Love
Pansy: Thoughts
Peach: Longevity
Peony: Aphrodisiac
Petunia: Soothing
Poppy: Imagination
Primrose: Youth
Rose: Love
Rosemary: Remembrance
Sage: Long Life
Strawberry: Perfect
Sweet Pea: Departures
Sweet William: Gallantry

Tulip: Fame
Violet: Modesty
Zinnia: Affection

gem-inspired baby names

Amber	Cameo	Emerald	Goldie	Jasper	Ruby
Amethyst	Coral	Garnet	Ione	Jewel	Sapphire
Beryl	Crystal	Gem	Ivory	Opal	Topaz
Bijou	Diamond	Gemma	Jade	Pearl	Tourmaline

SOME SOUND ADVICE

Although I love lockets, they do have a hollow sound when too many are on the same bracelet. The same goes for items like hollow shoes. If this type of thing annoys you, don't choose these sorts of charms.

🎀 COMPOSED BY AN ARTIST, THIS IS A LOVELY EXAMPLE OF A HAND-MADE CHARM BRACELET CREATED USING A RAINBOW OF COLORS AND RANDOM CHARMS FROM A JEWELRY BOX. (REBECCA PURCELL)

🎀 LOVELY GEM FLOWER CHARMS. (CENTER: ANONYMOUS. OTHERS: TRACEY ZABAR)

PUTTING IT ALL TOGETHER

Once you've chosen a bracelet and amassed a collection of charms to put on it, you'll need to decide on a layout. Then you need to find a reputable jeweler to assemble the bracelet for you and solder on each charm.

Arrange all the elements on a table as you think they should look. Spread the charms out evenly, leaving equal spaces for more charms you might add on later. Some bracelets have tiny charms on either side of the clasp, and each charm moving away from the clasp gets progressively larger, with the largest one in the middle of the bracelet. Other bracelets mix large and small so that they kind of zigzag around the chain. You can play around with the order a bit to see which charms look best next to one another. Remember: Anything piled on will naturally clink against its neighbors. If a charm is really precious and you are worried about chips, leave it off of a crowded bracelet. You can plan to put a charm on every link or every two or three links, or even three charms on the same link. As

long as the bracelet itself is strong enough to hold the charms, feel free to load them on as you please. If you keep piling the charms on, however, they will no longer hang down, but will stick up all over the place like a porcupine. It's a look. If you have dozens and dozens of charms and think the bracelet might be too heavy for you to wear, it probably will be. Consider making a second bracelet or editing out anything you don't just adore. The goal is to establish a rhythm that is pleasing to the eye. Take a digital photograph or make a color photocopy to document the order you finalize.

Next, if you don't already have one, you need to find a jeweler you can trust to assemble the bracelet for you. Choose someone who's been around for a long time; maybe ask any bejeweled friends you might have for recommendations. A jeweler who is honest, nice, and competent is worth a little extra money. Before you drop the bracelet at the jeweler, be 100 percent certain that the order of the charms you have established is really the look you want. Asking your jeweler to redo the bracelet can be an expensive change of mind—kind of like decorating your house all over again.

Take a copy of your digital photo or color photocopy along with you to the jeweler. This way, the jeweler will have a map of exactly what you want, and you will have a record of exactly what you left there. If a charm or stone disappears, it is easier to resolve the dispute with documentation, rather than relying on people's memories. Be clear about what you want done, and write any specific instructions on the photograph. In addition to communicating the work you

TOP: A MARVELOUS GOLD BRACELET COLLECTED BY THE LATE ROSEMARY "MICKEY" SULLIVAN PETERS. CHARMS INCLUDE A FOUR-LEAF CLOVER, FOR THE LUCK OF THE IRISH; THE POPE'S MITER, FROM A TRIP TO THE VATICAN; AN ILLUMINATED STATUE OF LIBERTY; TINY PLAYING CARDS IN A BOX; AND A LARGE DISK THAT SAYS, "TO THE ANGEL I MARRIED FOR 10 YEARS OF HAPPINESS." (TRISH PETERS) BOTTOM: A SILVER CHARM BRACELET GIVEN TO THE OWNER BY BRYANT GUMBEL, AS A THANK YOU FOR TWENTY YEARS OF WORKING AND TRAVELING TOGETHER. (TRISH PETERS)

DO want done, be sure to tell the jeweler if there are dents or engraving you DON'T want removed. One of the sweetest charms I ever saw is a little heart engraved with initials and all chewed up—it was used as the owner's teething ring. This is an example of a time when you want to keep the dings and dents in place. Make sure you put your name and telephone number right on the photograph or photocopy. DON'T forget to keep a duplicate copy for yourself. Always ask, and get in writing, how much everything will cost ahead of time.

I strongly, strongly recommend that you have your jeweler solder every charm onto the bracelet links. If you don't and you catch a charm on something, the suspension ring could stretch out and open and the charm would be lost forever. It might not be so easy to replace a charm from long ago or far away. Soldering can be an expensive undertaking, especially with multiple charms, but I can't stress its importance enough. Also critical is attaching a safety chain to your bracelet. Think of how devastated you'd be if you didn't take these simple precautions and you lost your bracelet. It's just too heartbreaking to contemplate.

A WONDERFUL GOLD CHARM BRACELET, WITH LOCKETS, PADLOCKS, AND ASSORTED CHARMS. (ROBIN DEUTSCH)

the family bracelet

This is the quintessential charm bracelet—you can't get more personal than marking your marriage and anniversaries, as well as the birth of children and grandchildren by adding charms. A family bracelet is a fun gift that keeps on giving from husbands to wives. The heirloom piece can then be divided amongst children.

BIRTH SYMBOLS: Birthstones, flowers of the month, zodiac signs, and the like, for every member of the family

FIGURES AND OBJECTS: Engagement ring, wedding bells, bride and groom, boys and girls, baby shoes, pacifiers, rattles, baby cups

SILHOUETTES: Boys' and girls' heads for each child or member of the family, cameos

TOP: IT'S A BOY, IT'S A GIRL, IT'S A BOY, IT'S A GIRL, IT'S A BOY, IT'S A GIRL. A STERLING SILVER BRACELET WITH ENGRAVED NAMES ON THE FRONT OF EACH CHARM AND BIRTH DATES ON THE REVERSE. (TRACEY ZABAR) BOTTOM: A BEAUTIFUL GOLD FAMILY BRACELET. (JANE HARNICK)

Be aware of the tintinnabulation a charm bracelet will make—for good karma, you might not want to wear your bracelet to a poetry reading, or to the office if you work in an open-plan space, or the library, or anywhere else where some semblance of quiet decorum is required.

Treat your charm bracelet as you would any expensive investment and store it where it will be safe and won't get scratched. If it is worth a ton of money, keep it in the bank vault, not in your jewelry box or underwear drawer. Insure it and store the insurance papers, along with a photographic record of the bracelet and a written list of each charm on it, as you would any precious papers, perhaps in a fireproof lockbox along with your birth certificates, passports, and such. This way, if the unspeakable happens and your charm bracelet is lost, you will have the insurance money and a photographic record so you will possibly be able to replace the piece.

Charms do tarnish, so treat your sterling silver bracelet as you would your fine flatware. They are a huge pain to polish yourself, and too many professional polishings can wear down details and engraving. Keep the bracelet in a tarnish-proof flannel bag. Gold tarnishes, too, especially low karat, as there is lots of copper mixed in. The look of an old, patinated gold bracelet is quite lovely. However, get your

80

A FINE GOLD BRACELET WITH A NUMBER OF SLIDES AND CHARMS, INCLUDING A LOVELY ENAMELED VIOLET PANSY AND A CHARM WITH A NATURAL PEARL. (ANONYMOUS)

bracelet cleaned if there is dust and grime or chicken grease on it. Never spray perfume or hair products near a charm bracelet, especially if there are charms with pearls, gems, or enamel. Fix little things that break and replace the missing stones.

MAINTAIN YOUR INVESTMENT

Check the strength of the clasp regularly. If it seems loose or pops open, get your jeweler to fix it immediately. This is worth the money, as is the safety chain I mentioned before. It is better to pay a little money for the sake of prevention than to watch your bracelet slide down the subway grating or to have it lying on the coatroom floor or in a snowdrift, vanished...

And if, despite all my warnings, your bracelet is gone forever; if you lost it, or it was stolen in 1962, or your evil cousin Thelma bamboozled it out of Grandma before you could get your own grubby paws on it, or if you never inherited one because there wasn't any money in the family, or nobody loved you enough to give you one, well, get over it, girl. Go out and buy yourself one. Spend as little or as much as you wish, but please, please have fun with it.

A MAGNIFICENT GOLD BRACELET WITH LARGE, BEAUTIFUL CHARMS, INCLUDING A LION'S HEAD WITH DIAMOND EYES, A GOLD DRUM INLAID WITH MOTHER-OF-PEARL, AND A GOLD AND PEARL BUNCH OF GRAPES. THE OWNER HAS SHARED MANY PAIRS OF HER GRANDMOTHER'S EARRINGS WITH HER SISTER AND DAUGHTERS. SOME OF HER SINGLE EARRINGS ARE ON THIS BRACELET. (ANONYMOUS)

the travel bracelet

Scouring the globe for charms every time you travel is a fantastic way to build an unusual bracelet. Charms make wonderful, relatively inexpensive souvenirs that are easy to pack and carry home. Plus, they help you remember where you have been. Pick up a few extras to give as gifts to other traveler friends. You may choose to stick with a theme (i.e., all silhouettes of states or all architectural landmarks) or just find something from every place you go. Some types and ideas:

BUILDINGS: Mini reproductions of the finest architecture a city or country has to offer—Buckingham Palace, the Duomo, the Vatican, La Scala opera house, the Parthenon, the Leaning Tower of Pisa, the House of the Seven Gables in Salem, Massachusetts, the White House

CULTURAL ICONS: A famous cultural contribution from the destination—a bust of Beethoven or Shakespeare, Michelangelo's David (fig leaf included), the Pietà

ENAMELED SHIELDS: Enameled with tiny images of places (most often in England and Germany), city or country crests, or motifs

LANDMARKS: Instantly recognizable things you won't find anywhere else—Paris's Eiffel Tower, New York's Statue of Liberty, Seattle's Space Needle, St. Louis's Gateway Arch, London's Big Ben, Copenhagen's Little Mermaid statue

REGIONAL SYMBOLS: Something a place is renowned for—a Japanese kimono, Austrian edelweiss, German beer stein, Swiss cuckoo clock, Chinese panda bear, Vegas slot machine, London phone booth

SILHOUETTES: Shapes of states, islands, countries, bodies of water

TRANSPORTATION: Airplane, cruise ship, double-decker bus, canoe, horse, donkey

SOUVENIRS OF PARIS. (LISA BIRNBACH)

WHERE I WENT ON MY SUMMER VACATION. A COLLECTION OF SILVER AND ENAMELED STATE CHARMS COLLECTED THROUGHOUT THE 1960S. (TRACEY ZABAR)

CHAPTER
4

beyond THE BRACELET

CLEVER THINGS TO DO WITH CHARMS

ONCE YOU'VE FOUND THE PERFECT READY-MADE CHARM BRACELET OR CREATED YOUR OWN, YOU MAY DISCOVER THE CHARM BUG IS STILL BITING AT YOU. THERE'S NO NEED FOR THE LOVE AFFAIR TO BE OVER. THERE ARE LOTS OF WAYS TO INCORPORATE SPARE CHARMS INTO EVERYDAY LIFE. FOR STARTERS, CHARM BRACELETS MAKE GREAT GIFTS FOR FAMILY AND FRIENDS. AND INDIVIDUAL CHARMS CAN BE USED TO EMBELLISH EVEN THE MOST MUNDANE ARTICLES SUCH AS SHOELACES OR A PLAIN T-SHIRT. READ ON FOR ENGAGING IDEAS ON HOW TO KEEP THE LOVE ALIVE.

○ TAKE AN ANNUAL PICTURE OF YOUR BABY GIRL WEARING A LITTLE CHARM BRACELET YOU'VE STARTED FOR HER. LET HER WEAR IT FOR

MARVELOUS GOLD CHARMS, MANY OF WHICH ARE MECHANICALS, COLLECTED OVER THE YEARS BY TERRY RODGERS. THIS BRACELET IS OFTEN WORN AS A NECKLACE, SUSPENDED ON THIS GOLD WATCH CHAIN. (TERRY RODGERS AND MELODY)

real when she's old enough not to swallow it or lose it.

○ Get over it if she loses it.

○ Take apart Grandmother's charm bracelet and put each charm on a new bracelet for every grandchild.

○ Slip three charms onto a safety pin, and wear them over your heart.

○ Make a charm bracelet for each of your sons, then put the bracelets away for their future brides or daughters.

○ Buy a box of candy, eat it, go on a diet, and fill the box with one charm for every five pounds you drop.

○ Engrave your name on ten silver hearts, ask your nine best friends to do the same, then trade them at a charm swap party.

○ During a long car ride, clip your charm bracelet onto your whining child's arm and you may get fifteen more minutes of peace. Just make sure the car windows don't open, and your little one isn't young enough to swallow any charms that might fall off.

○ Sew a sentimental charm onto a piece of your daughter's baby blankie once she outgrows it and save it in your jewelry box. When she goes to college, buy her a big, cozy down comforter, sew a tiny silk bag near the top, and tuck the piece of blankie and charm inside.

○ Slip a gold memento onto a silk cord and tie it around your wrist. An instant charm bracelet.

TOP: CHARMS ON A GOLD SAFETY PIN. (TRACEY ZABAR) BOTTOM: A BEACH BRACELET, WITH CHARMS STRUNG ON A CORAL-COLOR SATIN CORD. (SHLOMIT RUBIN)

TREAT YOURSELF—OR SOMEONE SPECIAL—TO A HEART-SHAPED CANDY BOX FILLED WITH CHARMS FOR VALENTINE'S DAY, AN ANNIVERSARY, A BIRTHDAY, A TUESDAY (YOU GET THE PICTURE). (TRACEY ZABAR)

○ Wrap silver fortune charms in parchment and bake in a cake for a bridal shower. Warn everyone if you do this. No one wants to make an emergency visit to the dentist for a chipped tooth.

○ Tie a bag of charms onto the Christmas tree for your daughter.

○ Have your favorite charm soldered onto the little place where your watchband connects to your watch.

○ Thread a charm onto your shoelace.

○ Give your child's teacher a red enameled apple charm on a silk cord.

○ Engrave a charm for your new puppy's collar.

○ Pin a loving cup charm that says "best boy" on your son's T-shirt the next time he breaks something, like his arm or another lamp.

○ When your best friend gets married, make a charm for her first anniversary that says, "And they said it wouldn't last." If they really said it wouldn't last, get something else.

○ Bring some charms to your friend's beach cottage for a house gift. Maybe you'll get invited back next year.

○ Make a locket with your child's photo inside for your baby sitter or housekeeper. If she hates kids, fire her instead.

 EXTEND THE CHARM BRACELET LOVE TO EVERY MEMBER OF THE FAMILY. THEY MAKE ADORABLE DOG COLLAR ACCENTS. ON THE LARGE DOG: A PERSONALIZED "LOUIS" COLLAR IN FAUX DIAMONDS, AND A PHOTO CHARM OF HIS HUMAN FAMILY. (COLLAR, ZACHARY, SARAH, AND HARRISON GALICKI. DOG, AARON FREIDUS) SMALL DOG: A CANINE-THEMED GOLD CHARM BRACELET WITH DOGS, BONE, DOGHOUSE, HYDRANT, AND LICENSE. (BRACELET, ROSIE ZABAR. DOG, AARON FREIDUS)

○ That bride doesn't need towels or a blender—she's been living with him for eleven years. Instead, organize a gift so each guest at the bridal shower chips in ahead of time for a charm bracelet. The bracelet could have the same number of charms as her guests. Everyone will cry, and she'll wear it down the aisle.

○ If you are the bride, give each attendant a charm bracelet. Don't forget your mother—and his.

○ Ask the tooth fairy to give your daughter one charm for each lost tooth.

○ Sew a silver heart onto your ponytail holder.

○ If that bracelet is just too heavy to wear, display it in a shadow-box frame.

○ Put all your extra charms on a necklace.

○ Slip a few inexpensive charms onto the ribbon of a birthday gift.

○ Create a new holiday called "Daughter's Day" as the antidote to Mother's Day and Father's Day. Yet another reason to spoil your princess!

○ Use cheap hoop earrings to make some wineglass charms.

ANY GIFT IS SWEETER WITH A COUPLE OF CHARMS TANTALIZINGLY DANGLING FROM THE RIBBONS. (SANDY GILBERT)

○ Buy the pinkest, purplest, girliest jewelry box for your daughter, slip a charm bracelet inside, and put it next to her pillow just before she wakes up on her ninth birthday.

○ Wear two or three charm bracelets at once.

○ Drop a charm attached to a ribbon into the batter of each cupcake for your daughter's birthday, and bake them with the ribbon hanging out. Each girl gets to pull out a wish.

○ Send a charm bracelet to your very best friend from kindergarten.

THREE LOVELY HAND CHARMS (LEFT AND RIGHT: TRACEY ZABAR, CENTER: ELLEN SILVERMAN)

GIVEN TO THE OWNER IN HIGH SCHOOL, THIS DELIGHTFUL GROUP OF CHARMS INCLUDES SCHOOL AWARDS, AN AMETHYST RING, AND A WORKING HARMONICA. (EMILIE KLAGSBRUN)

reading list

Becker, Vivienne, *Antique and Twentieth Century Jewellery,* New York: Van Nostrand Reinhold, 1982.

Bordenach Battalia, Gabriella, *Gioielli antichi dalla eta mirenea all'ellenismo,* Roma: Edizioni Quasar, 1980.

Breglia, Laura, *Catalogo delle oreficerie del museo nazionale di napoli,* Roma: Libreria dello stato, 1941.

Bury, Shirley, *Jewellery Gallery: Summary Catalogue,* London: Victoria & Albert Museum, 1982.

Bury, Shirley, *Sentimental Jewellery,* London: Victoria & Albert Museum, Her Majesty's Stationery Office, 1985.

Cartlidge, Barbara, *Twentieth-Century Jewelry,* New York: Harry N. Abrams, Inc., 1985.

Cologni, Franco, and Ettore Mocchetti, *Made by Cartier: 150 Years of Tradition and Innovation,* New York: Abbeville Press, 1992.

Cooper-Hewitt Museum, *Fabergé, Loan Exhibition for the Benefit of the Cooper-Hewitt Museum,* New York: The Smithsonian Institution's National Museum of Design, 1983.

Culme, John, and Nicholas Rayner, *The Jewels of the Duchess of Windsor,* London: Thames and Hudson in Association with Sotheby's, New York, 1987.

d'Orey, Leonor, *Five Centuries of Jewellery: National Museum of Ancient Art, Lisbon,* London: Zwemmer, 1995.

Fales, Martha Gandy, *Jewelry in America, 1600-1900,* Suffolk: Antique Collectors' Club, 1995.

Farneti Cera, Deanna, ed., *Jewels of Fantasy: Costume Jewelry of the 20th Century,* New York: Harry N. Abrams, Inc., 1991.

Farneti Cera, Deanna, *The Jewels of Miriam Haskell,* Milan: Antique Collectors' Club, 1997.

Field, Leslie, *The Queen's Jewels: The Personal Collection of Elizabeth II,* New York: Harry N. Abrams, Inc., 1987.

Flower, Margaret, *Victorian Jewellery,* London: Cassell & Co., 1951.

Garside, Anne, ed., *Jewelry Ancient to Modern,* New York: The Viking Press, 1979.

Gregorietti, Guido, *Jewelry: History and Technique from the Egyptians to the Present,* Secaucus, New Jersey: Chartwell Books Inc., 1979.

Gregorietti, Guido, *Jewelry Through the Ages,* New York: American Heritage, 1969.

Hinks, Peter, *Jewellery,* London/Melbourne: Paul Hamlyn Sun Books, 1969.

Hoffmann, Herbert, and Vera von Claer, *Antiker Gold–und Silberschmuck: Katalog mit Untersuchung der Objekte auf technischer Grundlage,* Mainz am Rhein, Hamburg: Verlag Philipp von Zabern, 1968.

Hughes, Graham, *The Art of Jewelry,* New York: Viking Press, 1984.

Jewellery Studies, Volumes 2 and 3, London: The Society of Jewellery Historians, 1985 and 1989.

Keay, Anna, *The Crown Jewels,* Surrey, U.K.: Historic Royal Palaces, 2002.

Kuntzsch, Ingrid, *A History of Jewels and Jewellery,* New York: St. Martin's Press, 1981.

Lanllier, Jean, and Marie-Anne Pini, *Five Centuries of Jewelry in the West,* preface by G. Boucheron, New York: Leon Amiel Publisher, 1983.

Lewin, Susan Grant, *One of a Kind, American Art Jewelry Today,* New York: Harry N. Abrams, Inc., 1994.

Luthi, Ann Louise, *Sentimental Jewellery,* London: Shire, 1998.

McConnell, Sophie, *Metropolitan Jewelry,* New York: The Metropolitan Museum of Art and Boston: Bulfinch Press/Little, Brown and Company, 1991.

Marchal Jewelry Catalog, New York: 1967.

Néret, Gilles, *Boucheron: Four Generations of a World-Renowned Jeweler,* New York: Rizzoli International Publications, 1988.

Ostier, Marianne, *Jewels and the Woman: The Romance, Magic and Art of Feminine Adornment,* New York: Horizon Press, 1958.

Phillips, Clare, *Jewelry: from Antiquity to the Present,* London: Thames and Hudson, 1996.

Phillips, Clare, *Jewels and Jewellery,* London: Victoria & Albert Museum, V&A Publications, 2000.

Ratton, Charles, *Fetish Gold,* Philadelphia: University Museum, University of Pennsylvania, 1975.

Ring, Betty, *Girlhood Embroidery: American Samplers & Pictorial Needlework, 1650-1950,* Volumes I and II, New York: Alfred A. Knopf, 1993.

Scarisbrick, Diana, *Ancestral Jewels,* London: Deutsch, 1989.

Scarisbrick, Diana, *Il valore dei gioielli e degli orologi da collezione,* Roma: Umberto Allemandi & Co., 1984.

Scarisbrick, Diana, *Jewellery,* London: Batsford, 1984.

Shields, Jody, *All That Glitters,* New York: Rizzoli International Publications, 1987.

Smith, H. Clifford, *Jewellery,* London: Methuen and Co., 1908.

Solodkoff, Alexander von, and G. von Habsburg-Lothringen, *Fabergé: Court Jeweler to the Tsars,* New York: Rizzoli International Publications, 1979.

Solodkoff, Alexander von, *The Art of Carl Fabergé,* New York: Crown Publishers, Inc., 1988.

Sotheby's, *The Diana Vreeland Collection of Fashion Jewelry Auction Catalog,* New York, October 21, 1987.

Sotheby's, *The Estate of Jacqueline Onassis Auction Catalog,* New York, April 23-26, 1996.

Sotheby's, *The Jewels of the Duchess of Windsor Auction Catalogue,* Geneva, April 2-3, 1987.

Tait, Hugh, and Charlotte Gere, *The Jeweller's Art, An Introduction to the Hull Grundy Gift to the British Museum,* London: The British Museum Publications Limited, 1978.

Taylor, Elizabeth, *Elizabeth Taylor: My Love Affair with Jewelry,* New York: Simon & Schuster, 2002.

Thompson, Kay, *Eloise in Paris,* New York: Simon & Schuster, 1957.

Untracht, Oppi, *Jewelry Concepts and Technology,* Garden City, New York: Doubleday, 1982.

Waterfield, Hermione, and Christopher Forbes, *Fabergé Imperial Eggs and Other Fantasies,* New York: Scribner, 1978.

Williams, Dyfri, and Jack Ogden, *Greek Gold: Jewelry of the Classical World,* New York: Harry N. Abrams, Inc., 1994.

Young, Sheila, *The Queen's Jewellery: The Jewels of H.M. Queen Elizabeth II,* New York: Taplinger Publishing Co., 1969.

AN EARLY NINETEENTH-CENTURY BRITISH EYE MINIATURE; WATERCOLOR PAINTED ON IVORY, WITH PEARLS SYMBOLIZING TEARS. (VICTORIA & ALBERT MUSEUM)

acknowledgments

My deepest appreciation goes to everyone who has been kind enough to share heirlooms and stories, who let me poke about in their jewelry boxes, vaults, and safes, and to all who wear my designs every day.

Thanks to Lisa Lebowitz Cader; Lisa Birnbach; my agent, Andy McNicol, and everyone at William Morris, especially Jennifer Rudolph Walsh and Joni Evans; Sandy Gilbert, my amazing editor, and everyone at Stewart, Tabori & Chang; Ellen Silverman, photographer extraordinaire; the brilliant Jen Cegielski; the talented Pamela Geismar; the Toback-Galicki family; Melody Rodgers; Robin Deutsch; Ellis Levine; everyone at Barneys New York, especially Stephanie Lee, Fatima d'Almeida, Gloria Lee and Judy Collinson; Pamela Bell, and everyone at Kate Spade; Whisper PR; Caroline Drabik at Sotheby's Jewelry Department; at Christie's, Emma Strouts and Sarah Hodgson; Josh Arfer; Stephen Plotkin, Frank Rigg, and Sharon Kelly at the John Fitzgerald Kennedy Library and Museum, Boston; Brooke Garber Neidich; Allison Sawczyn, Margaret Kelly Trombly, and Kip Forbes at the Forbes Collection; Martin Durrant from the Victoria & Albert Museum, London; Trish Peters; everyone at Mish, especially Laura; Stéphane Houey-Towner at the Costume Institute of the Metropolitan Museum of Art; the wonderful and amazing Lucie Arnaz; Phyllis Diller; Debbie Reynolds; Jerry Lewis; Connie Stevens; Joan Jakobson, Joyce Jonas, Karen Taffner Butler and Eleanor Taffner; and my family, Bill, Billy, Taylor, and Max Blumenreich.

To all already mentioned, and to Janice Adelson, Lauren Ambrose, Jennifer Aniston, Ann-Margret, Sue Ellen Appleman, Desi Arnaz, Courteney Cox Arquette, Brooke Astor, Lucille Ball, Barbara Barrie, Anna Baryshnikov, Sofia Baryshnikov, Judy and Neal Bergman, Linda Mitchell Koren at Betsey Bunky Nini, Emily, Lauren, and Samantha Boldt, Jane Bohan, Baby Jenny Bram, Boris Breuer, Matthew Broderick, Joan Burstein at Browns London, Mara Buxbaum, Michael Cader, Cynthia Carter, Louise Clare, Cleo, Bernard Cohen, Joanna Colbert, Carrie Cook Platt, The Cooper-Hewitt Museum, Arline Covell, Jamie Lee Curtis, Arlene Dahl, Hope Davis, Lorraine DeSalvio, Mrs. Fred DeCordova, Annie Santilli DeStefano, Margie Duncan, Dyckman's, Jill Egenberg, Mitchell Egenberg, David Faham, the Fashion Institute of Technology Library, Susan Fisher, Calista Flockhart, Devon Fredericks, David and Gail Friedman, Wendy Futterman, Allison Gardner, Debby Geltman, Jon Giswold, Carla Glasser, Julianna Glasser, Diane Goldsmith, Michael Goldstein, Grandma Rebecca, Dawn Hale, Mel Hanson, Christina Holmes, Debra Winger Howard, Helen Hunt, Peggy Intrator, Bessie Jamieson and Jewelry Arts Institute, Jean's Silversmiths, Jewelry Camp, Jewelry Information Center, Jeannette Judelson, Robin Kassimir, Liz Kehler, Steve Kerner, Rhonda Kirschner, Amy Lawch, Billy Lazarus, Janet Leigh, Fred Leighton, Ethel Lipsitz, Kusum Lynn, Carolyn Malinsky, Randie Malinsky, Alan Margulies, Shari Markbreiter, Donna Matsos, Joyce Mathias, the New-York Historical Society, Nancy Modica, Jami Moore, Julianne Moore, Lori Moore, Mary Tyler Moore, Harry Morgenthau, Martha Morgenthau, Ruth Mukherji, Elizabeth Mutnick, Nana and Nonnie, Amy Nederlander, Gwyneth Paltrow, Dr. Peggy Duffy Patterson, Stephen Pendergast, Pequita, Piper Perabo, Meryl Poster, Sue Poster, Dale Colantropo Pottie, Ethan Raduns-Silverstein, Shauna Redford, Janet Reilly, Penny Rice, Lisa Rinehart, Julia Roberts, Judy Rosenbloom, Amanda Joy Rubin, Gabrielle Sanchez, Emily Satloff, Natalie de Segonzac, Adele Seltzer, Rebecca Selva, Catherine Shimony, Manon Slome, A. Star Sorenson, Julia Stiles, Takashimaya, Fran Taylor, Charlize Theron, Karla Thomas, Marisa Tomei, Van Cleef & Arpels, Del Viarengo, Cathy Waterman, the Watson Library at the Metropolitan Museum of Art, Sigourney Weaver, Lottie Weber, William Jay Weber. Harry Loves Rosie.

And thank you to Sarah Jessica Parker (and Carrie Bradshaw).

A SWEET SIXTEEN BRACELET FROM THE 1960S WITH FINE GOLD CHARMS, INCLUDING ONE ENCASING A BRITISH TEN-POUND NOTE ENGRAVED "IN CASE OF EMERGENCY, BREAK GLASS." ANOTHER CHARM IS ENGRAVED, "TAKE HER, SHE'S MINE." (TRACEY ZABAR)

FRONT COVER: THE PERFECT GOLD BRACELET. (TRACEY ZABAR) PAGE 1: NURSERY RHYME BRACELET COMPOSED OF CELLULOID AND POSSIBLY BAKELITE BABY ANIMAL CHARMS, CIRCA 1940. (TRACEY ZABAR) PAGE 2: A STUNNING ART DECO PLATINUM BRACELET FEATURING "FRUIT SALAD" CHARMS: A PAVÉ AIRPLANE WITH GEMS SPELLING OUT THE WORD "DEAREST," A COWBOY WITH TWO SIX-SHOOTERS, A PRINCETON MAN, A PIANO PLAYER, AND A SAPPHIRE BIRD ON A SWING. (TERRY RODGERS AND MELODY) PAGE 4: THE PERFECT HUSBAND BRACELET. (TRACEY ZABAR)

BELOW: AN ENCHANTING COLLECTION OF HAND-CARVED REVERSE-PAINTED DOG INTAGLIOS. (BUSSMER CRYSTALS, D. PAGLIA AND SON)

Published in 2004 by
Stewart, Tabori & Chang
A Company of La Martinière Groupe
115 West 18th Street
New York, NY 10011

Canadian Distribution:
Canadian Manda Group
One Atlantic Avenue, Suite 105
Toronto, Ontario M6K 3E7
Canada

LIBRARY OF CONGRESS CATALOGING-IN-PUBLICATION DATA
Zabar, Tracey.
  Charmed bracelets / Tracey Zabar with Jennifer Cegielski ; foreword by Lisa Birnbach ; photographs by Ellen Silverman.— 1st ed.
    p. cm.
  ISBN 1-58479-334-1 (hardcover)
1. Charms (Ornaments) 2. Charm bracelets. I. Cegielski, Jennifer. II. Silverman, Ellen. III. Title.
NK4890.C47Z33 2004
739.27'8—dc22   2004009105

All uncaptioned charms property of Tracey Zabar.

PROJECT EDITOR: SANDRA GILBERT
PRODUCTION DIRECTOR: KIM TYNER
DESIGN: PAMELA GEISMAR

The text of this book was composed in ITC Garamond, Engravers Gothic, Engravers Bold Face, Trade Gothic, and Monterey BT.

PRINTED IN CHINA

10 9 8 7 6 5 4 3 2 1

FIRST PRINTING

Stewart, Tabori & Chang is a subsidiary of